CLASSIC
RECIPES™

Publications International, Ltd.

Pictured on the front cover: Classic Chocolate Cream Pie *(page 56)*.

ISBN-13: 978-1-4127-7740-7
ISBN-10: 1-4127-7740-2

Library of Congress Control Number: 2008928468

Manufactured in China.

8 7 6 5 4 3 2 1

Microwave Cooking: Microwave ovens vary in wattage. Use the cooking times as guidelines and check for doneness before adding more time.

Contents

COOKIES,
BROWNIES & BARS

Peanut Butter Cookies made with Hershey's Mini Kisses® BRAND Milk Chocolates

¼ cup (½ stick) butter or margarine, softened
¼ cup REESE'S® Creamy Peanut Butter
¼ cup granulated sugar
¼ cup packed light brown sugar
 1 egg
½ teaspoon vanilla extract
⅔ cup all-purpose flour
¼ teaspoon baking soda
⅛ teaspoon salt
1¾ cups (10-ounce package) HERSHEY'S MINI KISSES® BRAND Milk Chocolates

1. Heat oven to 350°F. Lightly grease cookie sheets.

2. Beat butter and peanut butter in large bowl with electric mixer on medium speed until creamy. Gradually add granulated sugar and brown sugar, beating until well mixed. Add egg and vanilla; beat until light and fluffy. Stir together flour, baking soda and salt; add to butter mixture, beating until well blended. Stir in chocolates. Drop batter by rounded tablespoons onto prepared cookie sheets.

3. Bake 10 to 12 minutes or until lightly browned. Cool slightly; remove from cookie sheet to wire rack. Cool completely. *Makes 18 cookies*

Peanut Butter Cookies made with Hershey's Mini Kisses® BRAND Milk Chocolates

7

Thick and Fudgey Brownies with Hershey's Mini Kisses® BRAND Milk Chocolates

2¼ cups all-purpose flour

⅔ cup HERSHEY'S Cocoa

1 teaspoon baking powder

1 teaspoon salt

¾ cup (1½ sticks) butter or margarine, melted

2½ cups sugar

2 teaspoons vanilla extract

4 eggs

1¾ cups (10-ounce package) HERSHEY'S MINI KISSES® BRAND Milk Chocolates

1. Heat oven to 350°F. (325°F. for glass baking dish). Grease 13×9×2-inch baking pan.

2. Stir together flour, cocoa, baking powder and salt. With spoon or whisk, stir together butter, sugar and vanilla in large bowl. Add eggs; stir until well blended. Stir in flour mixture, blending well. Stir in chocolates. Spread batter evenly in prepared pan.

3. Bake 30 to 35 minutes or until edges begin to pull away from sides of pan. Cool completely in pan on wire rack; cut into 2-inch squares.

Makes 24 brownies

Peanut Butter Glazed Chocolate Bars

¾ cup (1½ sticks) butter or margarine
½ cup HERSHEY'S Cocoa
1½ cups sugar
1½ teaspoons vanilla extract
3 eggs
1¼ cups all-purpose flour
¼ teaspoon baking powder
    Peanut Butter Filling and Glaze (recipe follows)
    Chocolate Drizzle (recipe follows)

1. Heat oven to 350°F. Line 15½×10½×1-inch jelly-roll pan with foil; grease foil.

2. Melt butter in medium saucepan over low heat. Add cocoa; stir constantly until smooth. Remove from heat; stir in sugar and vanilla. Beat in eggs, one at a time, until well blended. Stir in flour and baking powder. Spread batter evenly in prepared pan.

3. Bake 14 to 16 minutes or until top springs back when touched lightly in center. Remove from oven; cool 2 minutes. Invert onto wire rack. Peel off foil; turn right side up on wire rack to cool completely.

4. Prepare Peanut Butter Filling and Glaze. Cut brownie in half; spread half of glaze evenly on bottom half. Top with second half of brownie; spread with remaining glaze. Cool until glaze is set. Prepare Chocolate Drizzle; drizzle over glaze. After chocolate is set, cut into bars.

Makes about 40 bars

Peanut Butter Filling and Glaze: Combine ⅓ cup sugar and ⅓ cup water in small saucepan. Bring to a boil over medium heat. Remove from heat; immediately add 1⅔ cups (10-ounce package) REESE'S® Peanut Butter Chips. Stir until melted. Cool slightly. Makes about 1⅓ cups glaze.

Chocolate Drizzle: Place ⅓ cup HERSHEY₀S Semi-Sweet Chocolate Chips and 1 teaspoon shortening (do not use butter, margarine, spread or oil) in small microwave-safe bowl. Microwave at HIGH (100%) 30 seconds to 1 minute or until chips are melted and mixture is smooth when stirred.

Peanut Butter and Milk Chocolate Chip Studded Oatmeal Cookies

1 cup (2 sticks) butter or margarine, softened
1 cup packed light brown sugar
⅓ cup granulated sugar
2 eggs
1½ teaspoons vanilla extract
1½ cups all-purpose flour
1 teaspoon baking soda
½ teaspoon salt
½ teaspoon ground cinnamon (optional)
2½ cups quick-cooking oats
1 cup HERSHEY'S Milk Chocolate Chips
1 cup REESE'S® Peanut Butter Chips

1. Heat oven to 350°F.

2. Beat butter, brown sugar and granulated sugar in bowl until creamy. Add eggs and vanilla; beat well. Combine flour, baking soda, salt and cinnamon, if desired; add to butter mixture, beating well. Stir in oats, milk chocolate chips and peanut butter chips (batter will be stiff). Drop by rounded teaspoons onto ungreased cookie sheet.

3. Bake 10 to 12 minutes or until lightly browned. Cool 1 minute; remove from cookie sheet to wire rack.   *Makes about 4 dozen cookies*

Bar Variation: Spread batter into lightly greased 13×9×2-inch baking pan or 15½×10½×1-inch jelly-roll pan. Bake at 350°F. for 20 to 25 minutes or until golden brown. Cool; cut into bars. Makes about 3 dozen bars.

Hershey's Chocolate Mint Brownies

¾ cup HERSHEY'S Cocoa

½ teaspoon baking soda

⅔ cup butter or margarine, melted and divided

½ cup boiling water

2 cups sugar

2 eggs

1⅓ cups all-purpose flour

1 teaspoon vanilla extract

¼ teaspoon salt

1⅔ cups (10-ounce package) HERSHEY'S Mint Chocolate Chips

Glaze (recipe follows, optional)

HELPFUL HINT

For easy removal of brownies and bar cookies, line the baking pan with foil and leave at least 3 inches hanging over each end. Use the foil to lift out the baked treats; place them on a cutting board and carefully remove the foil before cutting into bars.

1. Heat oven to 350°F. Grease 13×9×2-inch baking pan.

2. Stir together cocoa and baking soda in large bowl; stir in ⅓ cup butter. Add water; stir until mixture thickens. Stir in sugar, eggs and remaining ⅓ cup butter; stir until smooth. Add flour, vanilla and salt; stir until well blended. Stir in mint chocolate chips. Spread batter evenly in prepared pan.

3. Bake 35 to 40 minutes or until edges begin to pull away from sides of pan. Cool completely in pan on wire rack. Drizzle glaze over top, if desired. Cut into bars. ***Makes about 36 brownies***

Glaze: Combine ⅔ cup powdered sugar and 2 to 3 teaspoons milk in small bowl; stir in a few drops green food coloring, if desired.

Peanut Butter Chip Fruit Bars

For easy serving of bars and brownies, remove a corner piece first; then remove the rest.

1½ cups REESE'S® Peanut Butter Chips, divided
1 package (8 ounces) cream cheese, softened
1 cup packed light brown sugar
1 egg
1 teaspoon vanilla extract
1 cup all-purpose flour
½ teaspoon baking soda
¼ teaspoon salt
½ cup quick-cooking oats
1 cup chopped dried mixed fruit or dried fruit bits
1 cup powdered sugar
2 tablespoons orange juice
¼ teaspoon freshly grated orange peel (optional)

1. Heat oven to 350°F. Grease 13×9×2-inch baking pan.

2. Place 1 cup peanut butter chips in microwave-safe bowl. Microwave at HIGH (100%) 1 minute; stir. If necessary, microwave an additional 15 seconds at a time, stirring after each heating, until chips are melted and smooth when stirred. Beat melted peanut butter chips and cream cheese in large bowl until well blended. Add brown sugar, egg and vanilla; blend well. Stir together flour, baking soda and salt; add to cream cheese mixture, blending well. Stir in oats, remaining ½ cup peanut butter chips and dried fruit. Spread batter evenly in prepared pan.

3. Bake 20 to 25 minutes or until golden brown. Cool in pan on wire rack.

4. Meanwhile, stir together powdered sugar, orange juice and grated orange peel, if desired, in small bowl; blend until smooth. (Add additional orange juice, a teaspoonful at a time, if glaze is too thick.) Pour over top and cool completely. Cut into bars.

Makes 2 dozen bars

When reusing the same cookie sheets for several batches, cool the sheets completely before placing dough on them. Dough will soften and begin to spread on a hot sheet.

Hershey's Special Dark™ Chips and Macadamia Nut Cookies

    6 tablespoons butter, softened
 1/3 cup butter-flavored shortening
 1/2 cup packed light brown sugar
 1/3 cup granulated sugar
    1 egg
 1 1/2 teaspoons vanilla extract
 1 1/3 cups all-purpose flour
 1/2 teaspoon baking soda
 1/2 teaspoon salt
 1 1/3 cups (8-ounce package) HERSHEY'S SPECIAL DARK™ Chips and Macadamia Nuts

1. Heat oven to 350°F.

2. Beat butter and shortening in large bowl until well blended. Add brown sugar and granulated sugar; beat thoroughly. Add egg and vanilla, beating until well blended. Stir together flour, baking soda and salt; gradually beat into butter mixture. Stir in chips and nuts. Drop by rounded teaspoons onto ungreased cookie sheets.

3. Bake 10 to 12 minutes or until edges are lightly browned. Cool slightly; remove from cookie sheets to wire rack. Cool completely.

Makes about 3 1/2 dozen cookies

White Chips and Macadamia Nuts Variation: Substitute 1 1/3 cups (8-ounce package) HERSHEY'S Premier White Chips and Macadamia Nuts for HERSHEY'S SPECIAL DARK™ Chips and Macadamia Nuts. Prepare as directed above.

Chocolate Cookie Variation: Decrease flour to 1 cup; add 1/3 cup HERSHEY'S Cocoa or HERSHEY'S SPECIAL DARK™ Cocoa. Prepare as directed above.

Chocolate-Almond Honeys

Chocolate-Almond Honeys

1¾ cups graham cracker crumbs
1 can (14 ounces) sweetened condensed milk
    (not evaporated milk)
2 tablespoons honey
2 tablespoons orange or apple juice
1 teaspoon freshly grated orange peel
1 cup HERSHEY'S Semi-Sweet Chocolate Chips
½ cup chopped blanched almonds

1. Heat oven to 350°F. Grease 9-inch square baking pan.

2. Stir together graham cracker crumbs, sweetened condensed milk, honey, orange juice and orange peel in large bowl. Stir in chocolate chips and almonds. Spread batter evenly in prepared pan.

3. Bake 30 minutes or until golden brown. Cool completely in pan on wire rack. Cut into bars. *Makes about 20 bars*

Peanut Butter Fudge Brownie Bars

1 cup (2 sticks) butter or margarine, melted
1½ cups sugar
2 eggs
1 teaspoon vanilla extract
1¼ cups all-purpose flour
⅔ cup HERSHEY'S Cocoa
¼ cup milk
1¼ cups chopped pecans or walnuts, divided
1⅔ cups (10-ounce package) REESE'S® Peanut Butter Chips
½ cup (1 stick) butter or margarine
1 can (14 ounces) sweetened condensed milk
    (not evaporated milk)
¼ cup HERSHEY'S Semi-Sweet Chocolate Chips

1. Heat oven to 350°F. Grease 13×9×2-inch baking pan.

2. Beat melted butter, sugar, eggs and vanilla in large bowl with electric mixer on medium speed until well blended. Add flour, cocoa and milk; beat until blended. Stir in 1 cup nuts. Spread evenly in prepared pan.

3. Bake 25 to 30 minutes or just until edges begin to pull away from sides of pan. Cool completely in pan on wire rack.

4. Melt peanut butter chips and ½ cup butter in medium saucepan over low heat, stirring constantly. Add sweetened condensed milk, stirring until smooth; pour over baked layer.

5. Place chocolate chips in small microwave-safe bowl. Microwave at HIGH (100%) 45 seconds or just until chips are melted when stirred. Drizzle bars with melted chocolate; sprinkle with remaining ¼ cup nuts. Refrigerate 1 hour or until firm. Cut into bars. Cover and refrigerate leftover bars.   *Makes 3 dozen bars*

California Chocolate Bars

6 tablespoons butter or margarine, softened
½ cup granulated sugar
¼ cup packed light brown sugar
1 egg
1 teaspoon freshly grated orange peel
1 teaspoon vanilla extract
1 cup all-purpose flour
½ teaspoon baking soda
¼ teaspoon salt
½ cup chopped dried apricots
½ cup coarsely chopped walnuts
1 cup HERSHEY'S MINI KISSES® BRAND Milk Chocolates
Milk Chocolate Glaze (recipe follows, optional)

1. Heat oven to 350°F. Grease 9-inch square baking pan.

2. Beat butter, granulated sugar, brown sugar and egg in large bowl until fluffy. Add orange peel and vanilla; beat until blended. Stir together flour, baking soda and salt; add to orange mixture. Stir in apricots, walnuts and chocolates. Spread evenly in prepared pan.

3. Bake 25 to 30 minutes or until lightly browned and edges begin to pull away from sides of pan. Cool completely in pan on wire rack. Prepare Milk Chocolate Glaze, if desired; drizzle over top. Allow to set; cut into bars.   *Makes about 16 bars*

Milk Chocolate Glaze: Place ¼ cup HERSHEY'S MINI KISSES® BRAND Milk Chocolates and ¾ teaspoon shortening (do not use butter, margarine, spread or oil) in small microwave-safe bowl. Microwave at HIGH (100%) 45 seconds or until chocolates are melted and mixture is smooth when stirred.

Chewy Chocolate Macaroons

Chewy Chocolate Macaroons

5⅓ cups MOUNDS® Sweetened Coconut Flakes
½ cup HERSHEY'S Cocoa
1 can (14 ounces) sweetened condensed milk
   (not evaporated milk)
2 teaspoons vanilla extract
   About 24 red candied cherries, halved

HELPFUL HINT

Maraschino cherries are sweet cherries that are pitted, soaked in sugar syrup, flavored and dyed a vivid red or green.

1. Heat oven to 350°F. Generously grease cookie sheets.

2. Stir together coconut and cocoa in large bowl; stir in sweetened condensed milk and vanilla until well blended. Drop by rounded teaspoons onto prepared cookie sheets. Press cherry half into center of each cookie.

3. Bake 8 to 10 minutes or until almost set. Immediately remove from cookie sheet to wire rack. Cool completely. Store loosely covered at room temperature.   ***Makes about 4 dozen cookies***

Prep Time: 15 minutes
Bake Time: 8 minutes
Cool Time: 1 hour

Peanut Butter and Milk Chocolate Chip Brownie Bars

6 tablespoons butter or margarine, melted

1 1/4 cups sugar

2 teaspoons vanilla extract, divided

3 eggs

1 cup plus 2 tablespoons all-purpose flour

1/3 cup HERSHEY'S Cocoa

1/2 teaspoon baking powder

1/2 teaspoon salt

1 can (14 ounces) sweetened condensed milk (not evaporated milk)

1/2 cup REESE'S® Peanut Butter

1 cup HERSHEY'S Milk Chocolate Chips, divided

1 cup REESE'S® Peanut Butter Chips, divided

3/4 teaspoon shortening (do not use butter, margarine, spread or oil)

1. Heat oven to 350°F. Grease 13×9×2-inch baking pan.

2. Stir together butter, sugar and 1 teaspoon vanilla in large bowl. Add 2 eggs; stir until blended. Stir together flour, cocoa, baking powder and salt; add to egg mixture, stirring until well blended. Spread evenly in prepared pan. Bake 20 minutes.

3. Meanwhile, stir together sweetened condensed milk, peanut butter, remaining egg and remaining 1 teaspoon vanilla. Pour evenly over baked layer. Set aside 1 tablespoon *each* milk chocolate chips and peanut butter chips; sprinkle remaining chips over peanut butter mixture. Return to oven; continue baking 20 to 25 minutes or until peanut butter layer is set and edges begin to brown. Cool completely in pan on wire rack.

Peanut Butter and Milk Chocolate Chip Brownie Bars

4. Stir together remaining milk chocolate chips, remaining peanut butter chips and shortening in small microwave-safe bowl. Microwave at HIGH (100%) 30 seconds; stir. If necessary, microwave at HIGH an additional 15 seconds at a time, stirring after each heating, until chips are melted and mixture is smooth when stirred. Drizzle over top of bars. When drizzle is firm, cut into bars. Store loosely covered at room temperature.   *Makes about 3 dozen bars*

CAKES
& CHEESECAKES

Celebration Chocolate Mini Cupcakes

¾ cup all-purpose flour

½ cup sugar

2 tablespoons HERSHEY'S Cocoa

½ teaspoon baking soda

¼ teaspoon salt

½ cup water

3 tablespoons vegetable oil

1½ teaspoons white vinegar

½ teaspoon vanilla extract

Celebration Chocolate Frosting (recipe follows)

1. Heat oven to 350°F. Line 28 mini (1¾-inch) muffin cups with paper liners.

2. Stir together flour, sugar, cocoa, baking soda and salt in medium bowl. Add water, oil, vinegar and vanilla; beat with electric mixer on medium speed until well blended. Fill muffin cups ⅔ full with batter.

3. Bake 11 to 13 minutes or until wooden pick inserted into centers comes out clean. Remove from pan to wire rack. Cool completely. Frost with Celebration Chocolate Frosting. Garnish as desired.

Makes 28 mini cupcakes

continued on page 26

Celebration Chocolate Mini Cupcakes

Celebration Chocolate Mini Cupcakes, continued

Celebration Chocolate Frosting

    1 cup powdered sugar
    3 tablespoons HERSHEY'S Cocoa
    3 tablespoons butter or margarine, softened
    2 tablespoons water or milk
    ½ teaspoon vanilla extract

Stir together powdered sugar and cocoa. Beat butter and ½ cup cocoa mixture in medium bowl until blended. Add remaining cocoa mixture, water and vanilla; beat to spreading consistency.

Makes about 1 cup frosting

Creamy Cinnamon Chips Cheesecake

    1½ cups graham cracker crumbs
    1 cup plus 2 tablespoons sugar, divided
    5 tablespoons butter or margarine, melted
    2 packages (8 ounces each) cream cheese, softened
    1 teaspoon vanilla extract
    3 cartons (8 ounces each) sour cream
    3 eggs, slightly beaten
    1⅔ cups (10-ounce package) HERSHEY'S Cinnamon Chips, divided
    1 teaspoon shortening (do not use butter, margarine, spread or oil)

1. Heat oven to 325°F. Combine graham cracker crumbs, 2 tablespoons sugar and melted butter in medium bowl. Press crumb mixture evenly onto bottom and about 1½ inches up side of ungreased 9-inch springform pan. Bake 8 minutes. Remove from oven.

2. Increase oven temperature to 350°F. Beat cream cheese, remaining 1 cup sugar and vanilla with electric mixer on medium speed until well blended. Add sour cream; beat on low speed until blended. Add eggs; beat on low speed just until blended. Do not overbeat.

3. Pour half of filling into prepared crust. Sprinkle 1⅓ cups chips evenly over filling in pan. Carefully spoon remaining filling over chips. Place on shallow baking pan.

4. Bake about 1 hour or until center is almost set. Remove from oven; cool 10 minutes on wire rack. Using knife or narrow metal spatula, loosen cheesecake from side of pan. Cool on wire rack 30 minutes more. Remove side of pan; cool 1 hour.

5. Combine remaining ⅓ cup chips and shortening in small microwave-safe bowl. Microwave at HIGH (100%) 30 seconds; stir until chips are melted and mixture is smooth when stirred. Drizzle over cheesecake; cover and refrigerate at least 4 hours. Cover and refrigerate leftover cheesecake. *Makes 12 to 14 servings*

Be sure to use the pan sizes specified in cake recipes. If the pan is too large, the cake will bake too quickly and possibly burn. If the pan is too small, the batter may spill over in the oven, causing not only a mess but a sunken middle as well.

Hershey's "Especially Dark" Chocolate Cake

2 cups sugar

1¾ cups all-purpose flour

¾ cup HERSHEY'S SPECIAL DARK™ Cocoa

1½ teaspoons baking powder

1½ teaspoons baking soda

1 teaspoon salt

1 cup milk

½ cup vegetable oil

2 eggs

2 teaspoons vanilla extract

1 cup boiling water

"Especially Dark" Chocolate Frosting (recipe follows)

1. Heat oven to 350°F. Grease and flour two 9-inch round baking pans.

2. Stir together sugar, flour, cocoa, baking powder, baking soda and salt in large bowl. Add milk, oil, eggs and vanilla; beat with electric mixer on medium speed for 2 minutes. Stir in boiling water (batter will be thin). Pour batter into prepared pans.

3. Bake 30 to 35 minutes or until wooden pick inserted into centers comes out clean. Cool 10 minutes; remove from pans to wire racks. Cool completely. Frost with "Especially Dark" Chocolate Frosting.

Makes 10 to 12 servings

"Especially Dark" Chocolate Frosting

½ cup (1 stick) butter or margarine

⅔ cup HERSHEY᾽S SPECIAL DARK™ Cocoa

3 cups powdered sugar

⅓ cup milk

1 teaspoon vanilla extract

Melt butter. Stir in cocoa. Alternately add powdered sugar and milk, beating to spreading consistency. Add small amount additional milk, if needed. Stir in vanilla.   ***Makes about 2 cups frosting***

Brownie Bottomed Peanut Butter and Milk Chocolate Chip Cheesecake

1 cup HERSHEY'S Milk Chocolate Chips, divided
1 cup REESE'S® Peanut Butter Chips, divided
6 tablespoons butter or margarine, melted
1 ¼ cups sugar
1 teaspoon vanilla extract
2 eggs
1 cup plus 2 tablespoons all-purpose flour
⅓ cup HERSHEY'S Cocoa
½ teaspoon baking powder
½ teaspoon salt
Cheesecake Layer (recipe follows)
½ teaspoon shortening (do not use butter, margarine, spread or oil)

1. Heat oven to 350°F. Grease 9-inch springform pan. Set aside 1 tablespoon *each* milk chocolate chip and peanut butter chips for drizzle.

2. Stir together butter, sugar and vanilla in large bowl with spoon or wire whisk. Add eggs; stir until well blended. Stir in flour, cocoa, baking powder and salt; blend well. Spread in prepared pan.

3. Bake 25 to 30 minutes or until edges begin to pull away from side of pan. Meanwhile, make cheesecake layer.

4. Immediately after removing brownie from oven, sprinkle remaining chips over brownie surface. Spoon cheesecake mixture over chips. Return to oven; continue baking 45 to 50 minutes or until almost set. Remove from oven to wire rack. With knife, loosen cake from side of pan. Cool 2 hours; cover. Refrigerate 3 to 4 hours or until thoroughly chilled. Remove side of pan.

Brownie Bottomed Peanut Butter and
Milk Chocolate Chip Cheesecake

5. Stir together reserved milk chocolate chips, reserved peanut butter chips and shortening in small microwave-safe bowl. Microwave at HIGH (100%) 30 seconds; stir. If necessary, microwave at HIGH 15 seconds at a time, stirring after each heating, until chips are melted and mixture is smooth when stirred. Drizzle over top of cheesecake. Cover and refrigerate leftover cheesecake.   *Makes 10 to 12 servings*

Cheesecake Layer: Beat 3 packages (8 ounces each) softened cream cheese and ¾ cup sugar until smooth in large bowl. Add 3 eggs, one at a time, beating well after each addition. Stir in 1 teaspoon vanilla extract.

Hershey's Special Dark™ Snack Cake Medley

Cream Cheese Filling (recipe follows)
3 cups all-purpose flour
2 cups sugar
⅔ cup HERSHEY'S Cocoa
2 teaspoons baking soda
1 teaspoon salt
2 cups water
⅔ cup vegetable oil
2 eggs
2 tablespoons white vinegar
2 teaspoons vanilla extract
½ cup HERSHEY'S SPECIAL DARK™ Chocolate Chips
½ cup MOUNDS® Sweetened Coconut Flakes
½ cup chopped nuts

1. Heat oven to 350°F. Grease and flour 13×9×2-inch baking pan. Prepare Cream Cheese Filling; set aside.

2. Stir together flour, sugar, cocoa, baking soda and salt in large bowl. Add water, oil, eggs, vinegar and vanilla; beat with electric mixer on medium speed 2 minutes or until well blended. Pour 3 cups batter into prepared pan. Gently drop cream cheese filling onto batter by heaping teaspoonfuls. Carefully spoon remaining batter over filling. Combine chocolate chips, coconut and nuts; sprinkle over top of batter.

3. Bake 50 to 55 minutes or until wooden pick inserted into cake center comes out almost clean and cake starts to crack slightly. Cool completely in pan on wire rack. Cover and refrigerate leftover cake.

Makes 12 to 16 servings

Cream Cheese Filling

HELPFUL HINT

½ cup HERSHEY'S SPECIAL DARK™ Chocolate Chips
1 package (8 ounces) cream cheese, softened
⅓ cup sugar
1 egg
½ teaspoon vanilla extract

To soften cream cheese quickly, remove it from the wrapper and place it on a medium microwavable plate. Microwave on MEDIUM (50%) 15 to 20 seconds or until slightly softened.

1. Place chocolate chips in small microwave-safe bowl. Microwave at HIGH (100%) 1 minute; stir. If necessary, microwave an additional 15 seconds at a time, stirring after each heating, until chips are melted and smooth when stirred.

2. Beat cream cheese and sugar in medium bowl until well blended. Beat in egg and vanilla. Add melted chocolate, beating until well blended.

Chocolate Orange Cheesecake Bars

CRUST

1 cup all-purpose flour
½ cup packed light brown sugar
¼ teaspoon ground cinnamon (optional)
⅓ cup shortening
½ cup chopped pecans

CHOCOLATE ORANGE FILLING

1 package (8 ounces) cream cheese, softened
⅔ cup granulated sugar
⅓ cup HERSHEY'S Cocoa
¼ cup milk
1 egg
1 teaspoon vanilla extract
¼ teaspoon freshly grated orange peel
Pecan halves (optional)

continued on page 34

Chocolate Orange Cheesecake Bars, continued

1. Heat oven to 350°F.

2. For Crust, stir together flour, brown sugar and cinnamon, if desired, in large bowl. Cut shortening into flour mixture with pastry blender or two knives until mixture resembles coarse crumbs. Stir in chopped pecans. Reserve ¾ cup crust mixture. Press remaining mixture firmly onto bottom of ungreased 9-inch square baking pan. Bake 10 minutes or until lightly browned.

3. For Chocolate Orange Filling, beat cream cheese and sugar with electric mixer on medium speed in medium bowl until fluffy. Add cocoa, milk, egg, vanilla and orange peel; beat until smooth.

4. Spread filling over warm crust. Sprinkle with reserved crust mixture. Press pecan halves lightly onto top, if desired. Return to oven. Bake 25 to 30 minutes or until lightly browned. Cool; cut into bars. Cover and refrigerate leftover bars.   *Makes 2 dozen bars*

Toffee-Topped Pineapple Upside-Down Cakes

4 tablespoons light corn syrup
¼ cup (½ stick) butter or margarine, melted
1 cup HEATH® BITS 'O BRICKLE® Toffee Bits
4 pineapple rings
4 maraschino cherries
¼ cup (½ stick) butter or margarine, softened
⅔ cup sugar
1 egg
1 tablespoon rum *or* 1 teaspoon rum extract
1⅓ cups all-purpose flour
2 teaspoons baking powder
⅔ cup milk

Toffee-Topped Pineapple Upside-Down Cake

1. Heat oven to 350°F. Lightly coat inside of 4 individual 2-cup baking dishes with vegetable oil spray.

2. Stir together 1 tablespoon corn syrup and 1 tablespoon melted butter in each of 4 baking dishes. Sprinkle each with ¼ cup toffee. Center pineapple rings on toffee and place cherries in centers.

3. Beat softened butter and sugar in small bowl until blended. Add egg and rum, beating well. Stir together flour and baking powder; add alternately with milk to butter-sugar mixture, beating until smooth. Spoon about ¾ cup batter into each prepared dish.

4. Bake 25 to 30 minutes or until wooden pick inserted in centers comes out clean. Immediately invert onto serving dish. Refrigerate leftover cakes. *Makes 4 (4-inch) cakes*

Chocolate should be stored in a cool, dry place (60° to 70°F.) When chocolate is exposed to varying temperatures, "bloom", a gray-white film, appears on the surface. It does not affect the taste and quality of the chocolate.

Hershey's Special Dark™ Truffle Brownie Cheesecake

BROWNIE LAYER

6 tablespoons butter or margarine, melted

1¼ cups sugar

1 teaspoon vanilla extract

2 eggs

1 cup plus 2 tablespoons all-purpose flour

⅓ cup HERSHEY'S Cocoa

½ teaspoon baking powder

½ teaspoon salt

TRUFFLE CHEESECAKE LAYER

3 packages (8 ounces each) cream cheese, softened

¾ cup sugar

4 eggs

¼ cup whipping cream

2 teaspoons vanilla extract

¼ teaspoon salt

2 cups (12-ounce package) HERSHEY'S SPECIAL DARK™ Chocolate Chips, divided

½ teaspoon shortening (do not use butter, margarine, spread or oil)

1. Heat oven to 350°F. Grease 9-inch springform pan.

2. For Brownie Layer, stir together melted butter, 1¼ cups sugar and 1 teaspoon vanilla. Add 2 eggs; stir until blended. Stir in flour, cocoa, baking powder and ½ teaspoon salt; blend well. Spread in prepared pan. Bake 25 to 30 minutes or until brownie layer pulls away from sides of pan.

3. Meanwhile, for Truffle Cheesecake Layer, beat cream cheese and ¾ cup sugar with electric mixer on medium speed in large bowl until smooth. Gradually beat in 4 eggs, whipping cream, 2 teaspoons vanilla and ¼ teaspoon salt until well blended.

Hershey's Special Dark™ Truffle Brownie Cheesecake

4. Set aside 2 tablespoons chocolate chips. Place remaining chips in large microwave-safe bowl. Microwave at HIGH (100%) 1½ minutes or until chips are melted and smooth when stirred. Gradually blend melted chocolate into cheesecake batter.

5. Remove Brownie Layer from oven and immediately spoon cheesecake mixture over brownie. Return to oven; continue baking 45 to 50 minutes or until center is almost set. Remove from oven to wire rack. With knife, loosen cake from side of pan. Cool 2 hours. Remove side of pan.

6. Place remaining 2 tablespoons chocolate chips and shortening in small microwave-safe bowl. Microwave at HIGH (100%) 30 seconds or until chips are melted and mixture is smooth when stirred. Drizzle over top of cheesecake. Cover; refrigerate several hours until cold. Garnish as desired. Cover and refrigerate leftover cheesecake.

Makes 10 to 12 servings

Brickle Bundt Cake

1⅓ cups (8-ounce package) HEATH® BITS 'O BRICKLE® Toffee Bits, divided

1¼ cups sugar, divided

¼ cup chopped walnuts

1 teaspoon ground cinnamon

½ cup (1 stick) butter or margarine, softened

2 eggs

1¼ teaspoons vanilla extract, divided

2 cups all-purpose flour

1½ teaspoons baking powder

1 teaspoon baking soda

¼ teaspoon salt

1 container (8 ounces) sour cream

¼ cup (½ stick) butter, melted

1 cup powdered sugar

1 to 3 tablespoons milk, divided

1. Heat oven to 325°F. Grease and flour 12-cup fluted tube pan or 10-inch tube pan. Set aside ¼ cup toffee bits for topping. Combine remaining toffee bits, ¼ cup sugar, walnuts and cinnamon; set aside.

2. Beat remaining 1 cup sugar and ½ cup butter in large bowl until fluffy. Add eggs and 1 teaspoon vanilla; beat well. Stir together flour, baking powder, baking soda and salt; gradually add alternately with sour cream to butter mixture. Beat 3 minutes or until blended. Spoon one-third batter into prepared pan. Sprinkle with half of toffee mixture. Spoon half of remaining batter into pan. Top with remaining toffee mixture. Spoon remaining batter into pan. Pour melted butter over batter.

3. Bake 45 to 50 minutes or until wooden pick inserted near center comes out clean. Cool 10 minutes; remove from pan to wire rack. Cool completely.

Brickle Bundt Cake

4. Stir together powdered sugar, 1 tablespoon milk and remaining ¼ teaspoon vanilla extract. Stir in additional milk, 1 teaspoon at a time, until desired consistency; drizzle over cake. Sprinkle with remaining ¼ cup toffee bits.   *Makes 12 to 14 servings*

Peanut Butter and Milk Chocolate Chip Layered Cheesecake

1½ cups graham cracker crumbs
⅓ cup plus 1 cup sugar, divided
⅓ cup HERSHEY'S Cocoa
¼ cup (½ stick) butter or margarine, melted
2 packages (8 ounces each) cream cheese, softened
1 teaspoon vanilla extract
3 cartons (8 ounces each) sour cream
3 eggs
1 cup HERSHEY'S Milk Chocolate Chips, divided
1 cup REESE'S® Peanut Butter Chips, divided
½ teaspoon shortening (do not use butter, margarine, spread or oil)

1. Heat oven to 325°F. Combine graham cracker crumbs, ⅓ cup sugar, cocoa and melted butter in medium bowl. Press crumb mixture evenly onto bottom and about 1½ inches up side of ungreased 9-inch springform pan. Bake 8 minutes; remove from oven. Cool slightly.

2. Increase oven temperature to 350°F. Beat cream cheese, remaining 1 cup sugar and vanilla with electric mixer on medium speed until well blended. Add sour cream; beat on low speed until blended. Add eggs; beat on low speed just until blended. Do not overbeat.

3. Pour 2 cups filling into prepared crust. Reserve 1 tablespoon each milk chocolate chips and peanut butter chips for drizzle. Sprinkle remaining milk chocolate chips and peanut butter chips evenly over filling. Carefully spoon remaining filling over chips.

4. Bake about 1 hour or until center is almost set. Remove from oven. Using knife, loosen cheesecake from side of pan. Cool on wire rack 30 minutes. Remove side of pan; cool 1 hour.

Peanut Butter and Milk Chocolate Chip Layered Cheesecake

5. Combine shortening and reserved milk chocolate chips and peanut butter chips in small microwave-safe bowl. Microwave at HIGH (100%) 30 seconds; stir. If necessary, microwave at HIGH an additional 15 seconds at a time, stirring after each heating, until chips are melted and mixture is smooth when stirred. Drizzle over cheesecake; cover and refrigerate at least 4 hours. Cover and refrigerate leftover cheesecake.

Makes 12 to 14 servings

PIES
& TARTS

Reese's® Peanut Butter & Hershey's Kisses® Pie

About 42 HERSHEY'S KISSES® BRAND Milk Chocolates, divided

2 tablespoons milk

1 packaged (8-inch) crumb crust (6 ounces)

1 package (8 ounces) cream cheese, softened

¾ cup sugar

1 cup REESE'S® Creamy or Crunchy Peanut Butter

1 tub (8 ounces) frozen non-dairy whipped topping, thawed and divided

1. Remove wrappers from chocolates. Place 26 chocolates and milk in small microwave-safe bowl. Microwave at HIGH (100%) 1 minute or just until melted and smooth when stirred. Spread evenly on bottom of crust. Refrigerate about 30 minutes.

2. Beat cream cheese with electric mixer on medium speed in medium bowl until smooth; gradually beat in sugar, then peanut butter, beating well after each addition. Reserve ½ cup whipped topping; fold remaining whipped topping into peanut butter mixture. Spoon over chocolate filling. Cover; refrigerate about 6 hours or until set.

3. Garnish with reserved whipped topping and remaining chocolates. Cover and refrigerate leftover pie. *Makes 8 servings*

Chocolate and Pear Tart

Chocolate Tart Crust (recipe follows)
2 tablespoons sugar
2 teaspoons cornstarch
1/8 teaspoon salt
1 cup milk
2 egg yolks, beaten
1 cup HERSHEY'S Semi-Sweet Chocolate Chips
Apricot Glaze (recipe follows)
3 large fresh pears, such as Bartlett or Anjou

1. Prepare Chocolate Tart Crust.

2. Combine sugar, cornstarch and salt in heavy medium saucepan; gradually stir in milk. Cook and stir over medium heat until thickened and bubbly. Cook and stir 2 minutes more. Remove from heat; gradually stir about half of hot filling into beaten egg yolks. Pour egg yolk mixture back into hot filling in saucepan; bring to a gentle boil. Cook and stir 2 minutes more. Remove from heat.

3. Immediately add chocolate chips, stirring until chips are melted and mixture is smooth. Pour into Chocolate Tart Crust. Refrigerate several hours or until firm.

4. Prepare Apricot Glaze. Core and peel pears; cut into thin slices. Place in circular pattern on top of filling. Spoon glaze over top of fruit, covering completely. Refrigerate several hours or until firm; remove rim of pan. Serve cold. Cover and refrigerate leftover tart.

Makes 12 servings

Chocolate Tart Crust: Heat oven to 325°F. Grease and flour 9-inch round tart pan with removable bottom. Stir together 3/4 cup all-purpose flour, 1/4 cup powdered sugar and 1 tablespoon HERSHEY'S Cocoa in medium bowl. Mix in 6 tablespoons cold butter or margarine with electric mixer at low speed until crumbly. Press evenly onto bottom and up side of prepared pan. Bake 10 to 15 minutes; cool.

Chocolate and Pear Tart

Apricot Glaze

¾ teaspoon unflavored gelatin

2 teaspoons cold water

2¼ teaspoons cornstarch

½ cup apricot nectar

¼ cup sugar

1 teaspoon lemon juice

HELPFUL HINT

Powdered gelatin will last indefinitely if it is wrapped airtight and stored in a cool, dry place.

1. Sprinkle gelatin over cold water in small cup; let stand 2 minutes to soften.

2. Combine cornstarch, apricot nectar, sugar and lemon juice in small saucepan; cook over medium heat, stirring constantly, until mixture is thickened. Remove from heat; immediately add gelatin mixture. Stir until smooth. *Makes about ½ cup glaze*

When cutting cream pies, the slices will cut better if the knife is wiped with damp cloth or paper towel between cuts.

Chocolate Macadamia Truffle Mousse Pie

9-inch baked and cooled pastry crust or packaged crumb crust (6 ounces)

1 ⅓ cups (8-ounce package) HERSHEY'S SPECIAL DARK™ Chips and Macadamia Nuts, divided

3 tablespoons plus 1 cup (½ pint) cold whipping cream, divided

1 teaspoon unflavored gelatin

1 tablespoon cold water

2 tablespoons boiling water

½ cup sugar

¼ cup HERSHEY'S Cocoa

1 teaspoon vanilla extract

Sweetened whipped cream or whipped topping

1. Set aside ⅓ cup chip and nut mixture. Place remaining mixture and 3 tablespoons whipping cream in medium microwave-safe bowl. Microwave at HIGH (100%) 1 minute; stir. If necessary, microwave at HIGH an additional 15 seconds at a time, stirring after each heating, until chips are melted and mixture is smooth when stirred. Spread mixture on bottom of prepared crust. Refrigerate.

2. Sprinkle gelatin over cold water in small cup; let stand 2 minutes to soften. Add boiling water; stir until gelatin is completely dissolved and mixture is clear. Cool slightly, about 5 minutes.

3. Meanwhile, stir together sugar and cocoa in small mixing bowl; add remaining 1 cup whipping cream and vanilla. Beat with electric mixer on medium speed until stiff, scraping bottom of bowl occasionally. Pour in gelatin mixture, beating just until well blended.

4. Carefully spread over chocolate layer. Cover; refrigerate several hours or until firm. Garnish with whipped cream and remaining chip and nut mixture. *Makes 6 to 8 servings*

Chocolate Macadamia Truffle Mousse Pie

Creamy Chocolate Tarts

⅔ cup HERSHEY₅S Semi-Sweet Chocolate Chips

¼ cup milk

1 tablespoon sugar

½ teaspoon vanilla extract

½ cup chilled whipping cream

6 (one 4-ounce package) single-serve graham cracker crusts
Sweetened whipped cream
Sliced maraschino cherries, fresh fruit, chilled cherry pie filling or fresh mint

1. Place chocolate chips, milk and sugar in small microwave-safe bowl. Microwave at HIGH (100%) 1 minute or until milk is hot and chips are melted when stirred. With wire whisk or rotary beater beat until mixture is smooth; stir in vanilla. Cool to room temperature.

2. Beat whipping cream until stiff; carefully fold chocolate mixture into whipped cream until blended. Spoon or pipe into crusts. Cover; refrigerate until set. Top with sweetened whipped cream. Garnish as desired. *Makes 6 servings*

Chips and Bits Cookie Pie

½ cup (1 stick) butter or margarine, softened

2 eggs, beaten

2 teaspoons vanilla extract

1 cup sugar

½ cup all-purpose flour

1 cup HERSHEY'S Semi-Sweet Chocolate Chips

½ cup HEATH® BITS 'O BRICKLE® Almond Toffee Bits

½ cup chopped pecans or walnuts

1 unbaked (9-inch pie) crust

Ice cream or whipped cream (optional)

1. Heat oven to 350°F.

2. Beat butter with electric mixer on medium speed in large bowl until fluffy. Add eggs and vanilla; beat thoroughly. Stir together sugar and flour; add to butter mixture, beating until well blended. Stir in chocolate chips, toffee bits and nuts; spread into unbaked pie crust.

3. Bake 45 to 50 minutes or until golden. Cool about 1 hour before serving; serve warm, or reheat cooled pie slices by microwaving on HIGH (100%) for about 10 seconds. Serve with ice cream or whipped cream, if desired.   ***Makes 8 servings***

Creamy Chocolate Tarts

Chocolate Strawberry Fruit Tart

1 ⅓ cups all-purpose flour

½ cup powdered sugar

¼ cup HERSHEY'S Cocoa or HERSHEY'S SPECIAL DARK™ Cocoa

¾ cup (1 ½ sticks) butter or margarine, softened

　Strawberry Vanilla Filling (recipe follows)

½ cup HERSHEY'S Semi-Sweet Chocolate Chips

1 tablespoon shortening (do not use butter, margarine, spread or oil)

　Glazed Fruit Topping (recipe follows)

　Fresh fruit, sliced

1. Heat oven to 325°F. Grease and flour 12-inch pizza pan.

2. Stir together flour, powdered sugar and cocoa in medium bowl. With pastry blender, cut in butter until mixture holds together; press into prepared pan.

3. Bake 10 to 15 minutes or until crust is set. Cool completely.

4. Prepare Strawberry Vanilla Filling. Spread over prepared crust to within 1 inch of edge; refrigerate until filling is firm.

5. Place chocolate chips and shortening in small microwave-safe bowl. Microwave at HIGH (100%) 30 seconds; stir. If necessary, microwave at HIGH an additional 15 seconds at a time, stirring after each heating, just until chips are melted and mixture is smooth when stirred. Spoon chocolate into disposable pastry bag or corner of heavy duty plastic bag; cut off small piece at corner. Squeeze chocolate onto outer edge of filling in decorative design; refrigerate until chocolate is firm.

6. Prepare Glazed Fruit Topping. Arrange fresh fruit over filling; carefully brush prepared topping over fruit. Refrigerate until ready to serve. Cover and refrigerate leftover tart. *Makes 12 servings*

Strawberry Vanilla Filling

  2 cups (12-ounce package) HERSHEY͵S Premier White Chips
  ¼ cup evaporated milk
  1 package (8 ounces) cream cheese, softened
  1 teaspoon strawberry extract
  2 drops red food coloring

1. Place white chips and evaporated milk in medium microwave-safe bowl. Microwave at HIGH (100%) 1 minute; stir. If necessary, microwave at HIGH an additional 15 seconds at a time, stirring after each heating, just until chips are melted and mixture is smooth when stirred.

2. Beat in cream cheese, strawberry extract and red food coloring.

Glazed Fruit Topping

  ¼ teaspoon unflavored gelatin
  1 teaspoon cold water
1½ teaspoons cornstarch or arrowroot
  ¼ cup apricot nectar *or* orange juice
  2 tablespoons sugar
  ½ teaspoon lemon juice

1. Sprinkle gelatin over cold water in small cup; let stand 2 minutes to soften.

2. Stir together cornstarch, apricot nectar, sugar and lemon juice in small saucepan. Cook over medium heat, stirring constantly, until mixture is thickened. Remove from heat; immediately stir in gelatin until smooth. Cool slightly.   *Makes about ¼ cup topping*

Upside-Down Hot Fudge Sundae Pie

⅔ cup butter or margarine
⅓ cup HERSHEY'S Cocoa
2 eggs
¼ cup milk
1 teaspoon vanilla extract
1 cup packed light brown sugar
½ cup granulated sugar
1 tablespoon all-purpose flour
⅛ teaspoon salt
1 unbaked 9-inch pie crust
2 bananas, peeled and thinly sliced
Ice cream, any flavor
Whipped topping

1. Heat oven to 350°F.

2. Melt butter in medium saucepan over low heat. Add cocoa; stir until smooth. Remove from heat. Stir together eggs, milk and vanilla in small bowl. Add egg mixture to cocoa mixture; stir with whisk until smooth and slightly thickened. Add brown sugar, granulated sugar, flour and salt; stir with whisk until smooth. Pour mixture into crust.

3. Bake 30 to 35 minutes until edge is set. (Center will be soft.) Cool completely, about 2 hours. Just before serving, top each serving with banana slices, ice cream and whipped topping.   *Makes 8 servings*

Upside-Down Hot Fudge Sundae Pie

Chocolate-Almond Pudding Tarts

¾ cup sugar

⅓ cup HERSHEY'S Cocoa

2 tablespoons cornstarch

2 tablespoons all-purpose flour

¼ teaspoon salt

1¾ cups milk

2 egg yolks, slightly beaten

2 tablespoons butter or margarine

¾ teaspoon vanilla extract

⅛ to ¼ teaspoon almond extract

6 single-serve graham cracker crumb crusts (4-ounce package)

Whipped topping

Sliced almonds

1. Stir together sugar, cocoa, cornstarch, flour and salt in medium microwave-safe bowl; gradually add milk and egg yolks, beating with whisk until smooth. Microwave at HIGH (100%) 5 minutes, stirring with whisk after each minute. Continue to microwave at HIGH 1 to 3 minutes or until mixture is smooth and very thick. Stir in butter, vanilla and almond extract. Spoon chocolate mixture equally into crusts. Press plastic wrap directly onto surface.

2. Cool; refrigerate several hours. Just before serving, garnish with whipped topping and sliced almonds. Cover and refrigerate leftover tarts.   *Makes 6 servings*

Chocolate Mint Mousse Pie

1 teaspoon unflavored gelatin
1 tablespoon cold water
2 tablespoons boiling water
½ cup sugar
⅓ cup HERSHEY'S Cocoa or HERSHEY'S SPECIAL DARK™ Cocoa
1 cup (½ pint) cold whipping cream
1 teaspoon vanilla extract
1 baked 8- or 9-inch pie crust, cooled
Mint Cream Topping (recipe follows)

1. Sprinkle gelatin over cold water in small cup; let stand 2 minutes to soften. Add boiling water; stir until gelatin is completely dissolved and mixture is clear. Cool slightly, about 5 minutes.

2. Meanwhile, stir together sugar and cocoa in medium bowl; add whipping cream and vanilla. Beat with electric mixer on medium speed until stiff, scraping bottom of bowl occasionally. Add gelatin mixture; beat just until blended. Pour into prepared crust.

3. Prepare Mint Cream Topping; spread over filling. Refrigerate about 2 hours. Garnish as desired. Cover and refrigerate leftover pie.

Makes 6 to 8 servings

Mint Cream Topping

1 cup (½ pint) cold whipping cream
2 tablespoons powdered sugar
¼ to ½ teaspoon peppermint extract
Green food coloring

Beat whipping cream, powdered sugar, peppermint extract and several drops green food coloring in medium bowl with electric mixer on medium speed until stiff.

Makes 2 cups topping

Classic Chocolate Cream Pie

5 sections (½ ounce each) HERSHEY₅S Unsweetened Chocolate
   Premium Baking Bar, broken into pieces
3 cups milk, divided
1⅓ cups sugar
3 tablespoons all-purpose flour
3 tablespoons cornstarch
½ teaspoon salt
3 egg yolks
2 tablespoons butter or margarine
1½ teaspoons vanilla extract
1 baked (9-inch) pie crust, cooled, or 1 (9-inch) crumb crust
   Sweetened whipped cream (optional)

1. Combine chocolate and 2 cups milk in large saucepan; cook over medium heat, stirring constantly, just until mixture boils. Remove from heat and set aside.

2. Stir together sugar, flour, cornstarch and salt in medium bowl. Whisk remaining 1 cup milk into egg yolks in separate medium bowl; stir into sugar mixture. Gradually add to chocolate mixture. Cook over medium heat, whisking constantly, until mixture boils; boil and stir 1 minute. Remove from heat; stir in butter and vanilla.

3. Pour into prepared crust; press plastic wrap directly onto surface. Refrigerate until well chilled. Top with whipped cream, if desired. Cover and refrigerate leftover pie. ***Makes 8 to 10 servings***

Classic Chocolate Cream Pie

Chocolate & Vanilla Swirl Tart

Tart Shell (recipe follows)
2/3 cup HERSHEY'S Semi-Sweet Chocolate Chips
1/2 cup milk, divided
2 tablespoons sugar
1/2 teaspoon unflavored gelatin
1 tablespoon cold water
2/3 cup HERSHEY'S Premier White Chips
1 teaspoon vanilla extract
1 cup (1/2 pint) cold whipping cream

1. Prepare Tart Shell.

2. Place chocolate chips, 1/4 cup milk and sugar in small microwave-safe bowl. Microwave at HIGH (100%) 1 minute; stir. If necessary, microwave at HIGH an additional 15 seconds at a time, stirring after each heating, just until chips are melted and mixture is smooth when stirred. Cool about 20 minutes.

3. Sprinkle gelatin over cold water in small cup; let stand 2 minutes to soften. Place white chips and remaining 1/4 cup milk in separate small microwave-safe bowl. Microwave at HIGH 1 minute; stir. Add gelatin mixture and vanilla; stir until gelatin is dissolved. Cool about 20 minutes.

4. Beat whipping cream in small bowl with electric mixer on high speed until stiff; fold 1 cup whipped cream into vanilla mixture. Fold remaining whipped cream into chocolate mixture. Alternately, spoon chocolate and vanilla mixtures into prepared tart shell; swirl with knife for marbled effect. Refrigerate until firm. Cover and refrigerate leftover tart. *Makes 8 to 10 servings*

Tart Shell

½ cup (1 stick) butter (do *not* use margarine), softened
2 tablespoons sugar
2 egg yolks
1 cup all-purpose flour

1. Heat oven to 375°F. Grease bottom and sides of fluted 8- or 9-inch tart pan with removable bottom.

2. Beat butter and sugar in small bowl until blended. Add egg yolks; mix well. Stir in flour until mixture is crumbly. Press onto bottom and up sides of prepared pan. (If dough is sticky, sprinkle with 1 tablespoon flour.) Prick bottom with fork to prevent puffing.

3. Bake 8 to 10 minutes or until lightly browned. Cool completely.

HELPFUL HINT

A frozen pie crust can be a lifesaver. Keep a couple in your freezer for last minute pies and desserts.

Easy Chocolate Coconut Cream Pie

1 (9-inch) pie crust

1 package (4-serving size) vanilla cook and serve pudding and pie filling mix*

½ cup sugar

¼ cup HERSHEY'S Cocoa or HERSHEY'S SPECIAL DARK™ Cocoa

1¾ cups milk

1 cup MOUNDS® Sweetened Coconut Flakes

2 cups frozen whipped topping, thawed

Do not use instant pudding mix.

1. Bake pie crust; cool completely.

2. Stir together pudding mix, sugar and cocoa in large microwave-safe bowl. Gradually add milk, stirring with whisk until blended. Microwave at HIGH (100%) 6 minutes, stirring with whisk every 2 minutes, until mixture boils and is thickened and smooth. If necessary, microwave an additional 1 minute; stir.

3. Cool 5 minutes in bowl; stir in coconut. Pour into prepared crust. Carefully press plastic wrap directly onto pie filling. Cool; refrigerate 6 hours or until firm. Top with whipped topping. Garnish as desired. Cover and refrigerate leftover pie.　　　　*Makes 8 servings*

NO-BAKE
DESSERTS

Fluted Kisses® Cups with Peanut Butter Filling

72 HERSHEY'S KISSES® BRAND Milk Chocolates, divided
1 cup REESE'S® Creamy Peanut Butter
1 cup powdered sugar
1 tablespoon butter or margarine, softened

1. Line 24 mini (1¾-inch) baking cups with paper liners. Remove wrappers from chocolates.

2. Place 48 chocolates in small microwave-safe bowl. Microwave at HIGH (100%) 1 minute or until chocolate is melted and smooth when stirred.

3. Using small brush, coat inside of paper liners with melted chocolate. Refrigerate 20 minutes or until set; reapply melted chocolate to any thin spots. (If necessary, chocolate can be reheated on HIGH for a few seconds.) Refrigerate until firm, 2 hours or overnight. Gently peel paper from chocolate cups.

4. Beat peanut butter, powdered sugar and butter with electric mixer on medium speed in small bowl until smooth. Spoon into chocolate cups. Before serving, top each cup with a chocolate piece. Cover and refrigerate leftover cups.   *Makes about 2 dozen cups*

For a richer chocolate flavor, substitute HERSHEY'S Semi-Sweet Chocolate Chips for HERSHEY'S Milk Chocolate Chips.

Milk Chocolate Pots de Creme

2 cups (11.5-ounce package) HERSHEY'S Milk Chocolate Chips
½ cup light cream
½ teaspoon vanilla extract
　Sweetened whipped cream (optional)

1. Place milk chocolate chips and light cream in medium microwave-safe bowl. Microwave at HIGH (100%) 1 minute or just until chips are melted and mixture is smooth when stirred. Stir in vanilla.

2. Pour into demitasse cups or very small dessert dishes. Cover and refrigerate until firm. Serve cold with whipped cream, if desired.

Makes 6 to 8 servings

Cool 'n Creamy Chocolate Pie

1 package (3 ounces) cream cheese, softened
¼ cup sugar
1 teaspoon vanilla extract
½ cup HERSHEY'S Syrup
1 cup (½ pint) cold whipping cream
1 packaged crumb crust (6 ounces)
　Sliced fresh fruit (optional)
　Chocolate curls (optional)

1. Beat cream cheese, sugar and vanilla in medium bowl until well blended. Gradually add syrup, beating until smooth. Beat whipping cream until stiff. Carefully fold into chocolate mixture. Pour into crust.

2. Cover and freeze until firm, about 3 hours. Just before serving, garnish with fresh fruit and chocolate curls, if desired.

Makes 6 to 8 servings

Milk Chocolate Pots de Creme

Easy Mini Kisses Choco-Cherry Pie

1 baked (9-inch) pie crust, cooled
1¾ cups (10-ounce package) HERSHEY'S MINI KISSES® BRAND
    Milk Chocolates, divided
1½ cups miniature marshmallows
⅓ cup milk
1 cup (½ pint) cold whipping cream
1 can (21 ounces) cherry pie filling, chilled
Whipped topping

1. Place 1 cup chocolate pieces, marshmallows and milk in medium microwave-safe bowl. Microwave at HIGH (100%) 1½ to 2 minutes or until chocolate is melted and mixture is smooth when stirred; cool completely.

2. Beat whipping cream in small bowl until stiff; fold into chocolate mixture. Spoon into prepared crust. Cover and refrigerate 4 hours or until firm.

3. Garnish top of pie with cherry pie filling, whipped topping and remaining chocolates just before serving. Refrigerate leftover pie.

Makes about 8 servings

Velvety Chocolate Mousse

1 teaspoon unflavored gelatin
½ cup cold milk
¾ cup (half 8-ounce bag) HERSHEY'S Sugar Free Chunks
¼ cup granular form sucralose*
2 teaspoons vanilla extract
1 cup cold whipping cream

Such as SPLENDA®, an artificial sweetener.

Velvety Chocolate Mousse

1. Sprinkle gelatin over cold milk in small saucepan; let stand 2 minutes to soften. Cook over medium heat, stirring constantly, until mixture just begins to boil.

2. Remove from heat; immediately add chocolate chunks, stirring until melted. Stir in sucralose and vanilla; blending until smooth. Pour into medium bowl; cool to room temperature.

3. Beat whipping cream until stiff; gently fold into chocolate mixture just until combined. Spoon into 4 individual serving dishes. Cover and refrigerate several hours or until firm. Garnish as desired.

Makes 4 servings

Fudgey Cocoa No-Bake Treats

2 cups sugar
½ cup (1 stick) butter or margarine
½ cup milk
⅓ cup HERSHEY'S Cocoa
3 cups quick-cooking rolled oats
⅔ cup REESE'S® Crunchy Peanut Butter
½ cup chopped peanuts (optional)
2 teaspoons vanilla extract

1. Line tray or cookie sheet with wax paper or foil.

2. Combine sugar, butter, milk and cocoa in medium saucepan. Cook over medium heat, stirring constantly, until mixture comes to a rolling boil. Remove from heat; cool 1 minute. Add peanut butter, oats, peanuts, if desired, and vanilla; stir to mix well.

3. Quickly drop mixture by heaping teaspoons onto wax paper or foil. Cool completely. Store in airtight container in cool, dry place.

Makes about 4 dozen

Prep Time: 20 minutes
Cook Time: 5 minutes
Cool Time: 30 minutes

Chocolate Nut Clusters

Chocolate Nut Clusters

1 cup HERSHEY'S Semi-Sweet Chocolate Chips

½ cup HERSHEY'S Premier White Chips

1 tablespoon shortening (do not use butter, margarine, spread or oil)

2¼ cups (11½-ounce package) lightly salted peanuts, divided

1. Place chocolate chips, white chips and shortening in small microwave-safe bowl. Microwave at HIGH (100%) 1 minute; stir. If necessary microwave at HIGH an additional 15 seconds at a time, stirring after each heating until chips are melted and mixture is smooth when stirred. Reserve ¼ cup peanuts for garnish; stir remaining peanuts into chocolate mixture.

2. Drop by teaspoons into 1-inch paper candy cups; top each candy with a reserved peanut. Refrigerate, uncovered, until chocolate is set, about 1 hour. Store in airtight container in cool, dry place.

Makes about 3 dozen candies

Deep Dark Mousse

¼ cup sugar
1 teaspoon unflavored gelatin
½ cup cold milk
1 cup HERSHEY'S SPECIAL DARK™ Chocolate Chips
2 teaspoons vanilla extract
1 cup cold whipping cream
Sweetened whipped cream (optional)

1. Stir together sugar and gelatin in small saucepan; stir in cold milk. Let stand 2 minutes to soften gelatin. Cook over medium heat, stirring constantly, until mixture just begins to boil. Remove from heat. Immediately add chocolate chips; stir until melted. Stir in vanilla; cool to room temperature.

2. Beat whipping cream with electric mixer on medium speed in large bowl until stiff peaks form. Add half of chocolate mixture and gently fold until nearly combined; add remaining chocolate mixture and fold just until blended. Spoon into serving dish or individual dishes. Refrigerate. Garnish with whipped cream, if desired, just before serving.

Makes 4 to 6 servings

Easy Chocolate Cheese Pie

4 sections (½ ounce each) HERSHEY'S Unsweetened Chocolate Premium Baking Bar, broken into pieces
¼ cup (½ stick) butter or margarine, softened
1 package (3 ounces) cream cheese, softened
¾ cup sugar
1 teaspoon milk
2 cups frozen whipped topping, thawed
1 packaged crumb crust (6 ounces)
Additional whipped topping (optional)

Easy Chocolate Cheese Pie

1. Place chocolate in small microwave-safe bowl. Microwave at HIGH (100%) 1 to 1½ minutes or until chocolate is melted and smooth when stirred.

2. Beat butter, cream cheese, sugar and milk in medium bowl until well blended and smooth; fold in melted chocolate.

3. Fold in 2 cups whipped topping; spoon into crust. Cover; refrigerate until firm, about 3 hours. Garnish with additional whipped topping, if desired. *Makes 6 to 8 servings*

Chocolate Dream Cups

1 cup HERSHEY'S Semi-Sweet Chocolate Chips
1 teaspoon shortening (do not use butter, margarine, spread
   or oil)
Chocolate Filling or Raspberry Filling (recipes follow)

1. Line 6 muffin cups (2½ inches in diameter) with paper liners.

2. Place chocolate chips and shortening in small microwave-safe bowl. Microwave at HIGH (100%) 1 minute; stir. If necessary, microwave at HIGH 30 seconds or until chips are melted and mixture is smooth when stirred.

3. Using a small pastry brush, coat insides of paper liners evenly with melted chocolate. Refrigerate 20 minutes or until set; reapply melted chocolate to any thin spots. (If necessary, chocolate can be reheated on HIGH for a few seconds.) Refrigerate until firm, 2 hours or overnight. Carefully peel paper from each chocolate cup. Cover and refrigerate until ready to use.

4. Prepare either Chocolate or Raspberry Filling. Spoon or pipe into chocolate cups; refrigerate until set. Garnish as desired.

Makes 6 dessert cups

Chocolate Filling

1 teaspoon unflavored gelatin
1 tablespoon cold water
2 tablespoons boiling water
½ cup sugar
¼ cup HERSHEY'S Cocoa
1 cup (8 ounces) cold whipping cream
1 teaspoon vanilla extract

1. Sprinkle gelatin over cold water in small bowl; let stand 1 minute to soften. Add boiling water; stir until gelatin is completely dissolved and mixture is clear. Cool slightly.

2. Stir together sugar and cocoa in another small bowl; add whipping cream and vanilla. Beat with electric mixer on medium speed until stiff, scraping bottom of bowl occasionally. Pour in gelatin mixture; beat until well blended.

Raspberry Filling

    1 package (10 ounces) frozen red raspberries, thawed
    1 teaspoon unflavored gelatin
    1 tablespoon cold water
    2 tablespoons boiling water
    1 cup (8 ounces) cold whipping cream
    ¼ cup powdered sugar
    ½ teaspoon vanilla extract
    3 to 4 drops red food coloring

1. Drain raspberries; press berries through sieve to remove seeds. Discard seeds.

2. Sprinkle gelatin over cold water in small bowl; let stand 2 minutes to soften. Add boiling water; stir until gelatin is completely dissolved and mixture is clear. Cool slightly.

3. Beat whipping cream and sugar in another small bowl until soft peaks form; pour in gelatin mixture and beat until stiff. Carefully fold in pressed raspberries and food coloring; refrigerate 20 minutes.

If fudge is difficult to cut into neat squares, place in refrigerator or freezer until firm. This will make it easier to cut.

Butterscotch Nut Fudge

1¾ cups sugar
1 jar (7 ounces) marshmallow creme
¾ cup evaporated milk
¼ cup (½ stick) butter
1¾ cups (11-ounce package) HERSHEY'S Butterscotch Chips
1 cup chopped salted mixed nuts
1 teaspoon vanilla extract

1. Line 8-inch square pan with foil, extending foil over edges of pan.

2. Combine sugar, marshmallow creme, evaporated milk and butter in large heavy 3-quart saucepan. Cook over medium heat, stirring constantly, until mixture comes to full boil; boil and stir 5 minutes.

3. Remove from heat; gradually add butterscotch chips, stirring until chips are melted. Stir in nuts and vanilla. Pour into prepared pan; cool.

4. Refrigerate 2 hours or until set. Remove from pan; place on cutting board. Peel off foil. Cut into squares. Store in airtight container in refrigerator. ***Makes about 5 dozen pieces or about 2¼ pounds candy***

Peanut Butter and Chocolate Mousse Pie

1 (9-inch) pie crust, baked and cooled
1⅔ cups (10-ounce package) REESE'S® Peanut Butter Chips, divided
1 package (3 ounces) cream cheese, softened
¼ cup powdered sugar
⅓ cup plus 2 tablespoons milk, divided
1 teaspoon unflavored gelatin
1 tablespoon cold water
2 tablespoons boiling water
½ cup sugar

Peanut Butter and Chocolate Mousse Pie

⅓ cup HERSHEY'S Cocoa
1 cup (½ pint) cold whipping cream
1 teaspoon vanilla extract

1. Melt 1½ cups peanut butter chips in small saucepan over low heat. Beat cream cheese, powdered sugar and ⅓ cup milk in medium bowl until smooth. Add melted chips; beat well. Beat in remaining 2 tablespoons milk. Spread in cooled crust.

2. Sprinkle gelatin over cold water in small bowl; let stand 1 minute to soften. Add boiling water; stir until gelatin is completely dissolved. Cool slightly. Combine sugar and cocoa in medium bowl; add whipping cream and vanilla. Beat with electric mixer on medium speed until stiff; add gelatin mixture, beating until well blended. Spoon over peanut butter layer. Refrigerate several hours. Garnish with remaining chips. Cover and refrigerate leftover pie.   ***Makes 6 to 8 servings***

Do not leave boiling sugar unattended. It can go from perfect caramel to totally burnt in just a few seconds.

Hershey's Special Dark™ and Macadamia Toffee Crunch

1⅓ cups (8-ounce package) HERSHEY'S SPECIAL DARK™ Chips
    and Macadamia Nuts
¾ cup (1½ sticks) butter
¾ cup sugar
3 tablespoons light corn syrup

1. Line 8-or 9-inch square or round pan with foil, extending foil over edges of pan; butter foil. Reserve 2 tablespoons chocolate chip and nut mixture; sprinkle remaining chip mixture over bottom of prepared pan.

2. Combine butter, sugar and corn syrup in heavy medium saucepan; cook over low heat, stirring constantly, until butter is melted and sugar is dissolved. Increase heat to medium; cook, stirring constantly, until mixture boils. Cook and stir until mixture turns a light caramel color (about 15 minutes).

3. Immediately pour mixture over chip and nut mixture in pan, spreading evenly. Sprinkle reserved chip mixture over surface. Cool. Refrigerate until chocolate is firm. Remove from pan; peel off foil. Break into pieces. Store in airtight container in cool, dry place.

Makes about 1 pound candy

White Chip and Macadamia Toffee Crunch: Substitute 1⅓ cups (8-ounce package) HERSHEY'S Premier White Chips and Macadamia Nuts for HERSHEY'S SPECIAL DARK™ Chips and Macadamia Nuts. Proceed as directed above.

White Chip and Macadamia Toffee Crunch

Chocolate Buttercream Cherry Candies

About 48 maraschino cherries with stems, well drained
¼ cup (½ stick) butter, softened
2 cups powdered sugar
¼ cup HERSHEY'S Cocoa or HERSHEY'S SPECIAL DARK™ Cocoa
1 to 2 tablespoons milk, divided
½ teaspoon vanilla extract
¼ teaspoon almond extract
White Chip Coating (recipe follows)
Chocolate Chip Drizzle (recipe follows)

1. Cover tray with wax paper. Lightly press cherries between layers of paper towels to remove excess moisture.

2. Beat butter, powdered sugar, cocoa and 1 tablespoon milk in small bowl until well blended; stir in vanilla and almond extract. If necessary, add remaining milk, one teaspoon at a time, until mixture holds together but is not wet.

3. Mold scant teaspoon mixture around each cherry, covering completely; place on prepared tray. Cover; refrigerate 3 hours or until firm.

4. Prepare White Chip Coating. Holding each cherry by stem, dip into coating. Place on tray; refrigerate until firm.

5. About 1 hour before serving, prepare Chocolate Chip Drizzle; with tines of fork drizzle randomly over candies. Refrigerate until drizzle is set. Refrigerate leftover candies. ***Makes about 48 candies***

Chocolate Buttercream Cherry Candies

White Chip Coating: Place 2 cups (12-ounce package) HERSHEY S Premier White Chips in small microwave-safe bowl; drizzle with 2 tablespoons vegetable oil. Microwave at HIGH (100%) 1 minute; stir. If necessary, microwave at HIGH an additional 15 seconds at a time, stirring after each heating, just until chips are melted and mixture is smooth. If mixture thickens while coating cherries, microwave at HIGH 15 seconds; stir until smooth.

Chocolate Chip Drizzle: Place ¼ cup HERSHEY S Semi-Sweet Chocolate Chips and ¼ teaspoon shortening (do not use butter, margarine, spread or oil) in another small microwave-safe bowl. Microwave at HIGH (100%) 30 seconds to 1 minute; stir until chips are melted and mixture is smooth.

Chocolate Magic Mousse Pie

1 envelope (about 1 ounce) unflavored gelatin
2 tablespoons cold water
¼ cup boiling water
1 cup sugar
½ cup HERSHEY'S Cocoa
2 cups (1 pint) cold whipping cream
2 teaspoons vanilla extract
1 packaged graham cracker crumb crust (6 ounces)
   Refrigerated light whipped cream in pressurized can
   HERSHEY'S MINI KISSES® BRAND Milk Chocolates

1. Sprinkle gelatin over cold water in small bowl; let stand 2 minutes to soften. Add boiling water; stir until gelatin is completely dissolved and mixture is clear. Cool slightly.

2. Mix sugar and cocoa in large bowl; add whipping cream and vanilla. Beat with electric mixer on medium speed until stiff, scraping bottom of bowl often. Pour in gelatin mixture; beat until well blended. Spoon into crust. Refrigerate about 3 hours. Garnish with whipped cream and chocolates. Cover and refrigerate leftover pie.

Makes 6 to 8 servings

Chocolate Magic Mousse Pie

HOLIDAY
CELEBRATIONS

Hershey's Special Dark™ Chips and Macadamia Nut Fudge

1¾ cups sugar

1 jar (7 ounces) marshmallow creme

¾ cup evaporated milk

¼ cup (½ stick) butter

2⅔ cups (two 8-ounce packages) HERSHEY'S SPECIAL DARK™ Chips and Macadamia Pieces

1 teaspoon vanilla extract

1. Line 8-inch square pan with foil, extending foil over edges of pan.

2. Combine sugar, marshmallow creme, evaporated milk and butter in large heavy 3-quart saucepan. Cook over medium heat, stirring constantly, until mixture comes to a full boil; boil and stir 5 minutes.

3. Remove from heat. Gradually add chips and nuts, stirring until chips are melted. Stir in vanilla. Pour into prepared pan; cool until set.

4. Remove from pan; place on cutting board. Peel off foil. Cut into squares. Store in airtight container in cool, dry place.

Makes about 5 dozen pieces or about 2¼ pounds candy

Chocolate Cranberry Bars

2 cups vanilla wafer crumbs (about 60 wafers, crushed)
½ cup HERSHEY'S Cocoa
3 tablespoons sugar
⅔ cup cold butter, cut into pieces
1 can (14 ounces) sweetened condensed milk
    (not evaporated milk)
1 cup REESE'S® Peanut Butter Chips
1⅓ cups (6-ounce package) sweetened dried cranberries
        or 1⅓ cups raisins
1 cup coarsely chopped walnuts

1. Heat oven to 350°F.

2. Stir together vanilla wafer crumbs, cocoa and sugar in medium bowl; cut in butter until crumbly. Press mixture evenly on bottom and ½-inch up sides of ungreased 13×9×2-inch baking pan. Pour sweetened condensed milk over crumb mixture; sprinkle evenly with peanut butter chips and dried cranberries. Sprinkle nuts on top; press down firmly.

3. Bake 25 to 30 minutes or until lightly browned. Cool completely in pan on wire rack. Cut into bars. Cover leftovers with foil. Store at room temperature. *Makes 3 dozen bars*

Chocolate Cranberry Bars

HELPFUL HINT

For best results, do not double this recipe.

Toffee Popcorn Crunch

8 cups popped popcorn
¾ cup whole or slivered almonds
1⅓ cups (8-ounce package) HEATH® BITS 'O BRICKLE® Almond Toffee Bits
½ cup light corn syrup

1. Heat oven to 275°F. Grease large roasting pan or two 13×9×2-inch baking pans. Place popcorn and almonds in prepared pan; toss to combine.

2. Combine toffee bits and corn syrup in heavy medium saucepan. Cook over medium heat, stirring constantly, until toffee melts (about 12 minutes). Pour over popcorn mixture; stir until evenly coated.

3. Bake 30 minutes, stirring frequently. Remove from oven; stir every 2 minutes until slightly cooled. Cool completely. Store in airtight container in cool, dry place.   ***Makes about 1 pound popcorn***

Holiday Double Peanut Butter Fudge Cookies

1 can (14 ounces) sweetened condensed milk (not evaporated milk)
¾ cup REESE'S® Creamy Peanut Butter
2 cups all-purpose biscuit baking mix
1 teaspoon vanilla extract
¾ cup REESE'S® Peanut Butter Chips
¼ cup granulated sugar
½ teaspoon red colored sugar
½ teaspoon green colored sugar

Holiday Double Peanut Butter Fudge Cookies

1. Heat oven to 375°F.

2. Beat sweetened condensed milk and peanut butter in large bowl with electric mixer on medium speed until smooth. Beat in baking mix and vanilla; stir in peanut butter chips. Set aside.

3. Stir together granulated sugar and colored sugars in small bowl. Shape dough into 1-inch balls; roll in sugar. Place 2 inches apart on ungreased cookie sheet; flatten slightly with bottom of glass.

4. Bake 6 to 8 minutes or until very lightly browned (do not overbake). Cool slightly. Remove to wire rack and cool completely. Store in airtight container in cool dry place.   *Makes about 3½ dozen cookies*

Pecans can be stored in an airtight container up to 3 months in the refrigerator and up to 6 months in the freezer.

Chocolate Pecan Pie

1 cup sugar
⅓ cup HERSHEY'S Cocoa
3 eggs, lightly beaten
¾ cup light corn syrup
1 tablespoon butter or margarine, melted
1 teaspoon vanilla extract
1 cup pecan halves
1 unbaked (9-inch pie) crust
   Whipped topping (optional)

1. Heat oven to 350°F.

2. Stir together sugar and cocoa in medium bowl. Add eggs, corn syrup, butter and vanilla; stir until well blended. Stir in pecans. Pour into unbaked pie crust.

3. Bake 60 minutes or until set. Remove to wire rack and cool completely. Garnish with whipped topping, if desired.

Makes 8 servings

Holiday Chocolate Fruit Cake

  1 package (8 ounces) cream cheese, softened
½ cup (1 stick) butter or margarine, softened
  1 cup sugar
  4 eggs
2¼ cups all-purpose flour, divided
  ⅓ cup HERSHEY'S SPECIAL DARK™ Cocoa
  1 teaspoon baking powder
½ teaspoon salt
½ cup orange juice
  2 cups coarsely chopped red candied cherries
1¼ cups golden raisins
1¼ cups pecan pieces
  1 cup HERSHEY'S MINI CHIPS™ Semi-Sweet Chocolate Chips
  2 tablespoons brandy *or* 4 teaspoons brandy extract plus
      2 teaspoons rum extract

1. Heat oven to 300°F. Grease and flour 10-inch tube pan.

2. Beat cream cheese, butter and sugar in large bowl with electric mixer on medium speed until blended. Add eggs, one at a time, beating until fluffy. Stir together 2 cups flour, cocoa, baking powder and salt; add to cream cheese mixture, alternately with orange juice, beating until well blended. Toss remaining ¼ cup flour with cherries, raisins, pecans and chocolate chips in small bowl; stir into cocoa mixture with brandy until blended.

3. Bake 1 hour and 30 minutes or until wooden pick inserted near center comes out clean. Cool 15 minutes; remove from pan to wire rack. Cool completely. Cover and refrigerate leftover cake. Garnish as desired.   ***Makes about 12 servings***

Chocolate Pecan Pie

This dessert is best eaten the same day it is prepared.

Toffee Bread Pudding with Cinnamon Toffee Sauce

1⅓ cups (8-ounce package) HEATH® BITS 'O BRICKLE® Toffee Bits, divided
3 cups milk
4 eggs
¾ cup sugar
¾ teaspoon ground cinnamon
¾ teaspoon vanilla extract
½ teaspoon salt
6 to 6½ cups ½-inch cubes French, Italian or sourdough bread
Cinnamon Toffee Sauce (recipe follows)
Sweetened whipped cream or ice cream (optional)

1. Heat oven to 350°F. Butter 13×9×2-inch baking pan. Reserve ¾ cup toffee bits for sauce.

2. Whisk milk, eggs, sugar, cinnamon, vanilla and salt in large bowl until well blended. Stir in bread cubes, coating completely. Allow to stand 10 minutes. Stir in remaining toffee bits. Pour into prepared pan.

3. Bake 40 to 45 minutes or until surface is set. Cool 30 minutes.

4. Meanwhile, prepare Cinnamon Toffee Sauce. Cut pudding into squares; top with sauce and sweetened whipped cream or ice cream, if desired.   *Makes 12 servings*

Cinnamon Toffee Sauce: Combine ¾ cup reserved toffee bits, ⅓ cup whipping cream and ⅛ teaspoon ground cinnamon in medium saucepan. Cook over low heat, stirring constantly, until toffee melts and mixture is well blended. (As toffee melts, small bits of almond will remain.) Makes about ⅔ cup sauce.

Hershey's Chocolate Peppermint Roll

CHOCOLATE SPONGE ROLL

4 eggs, separated
½ cup plus ⅓ cup granulated sugar, divided
1 teaspoon vanilla extract
½ cup all-purpose flour
⅓ cup HERSHEY'S Cocoa
½ teaspoon baking powder
¼ teaspoon baking soda
⅛ teaspoon salt
⅓ cup water

PEPPERMINT FILLING

1 cup whipping cream, cold
¼ cup powdered sugar
¼ cup finely crushed hard peppermint candy *or* ½ teaspoon
    mint extract
Few drops red food coloring (optional)

CHOCOLATE GLAZE

2 tablespoons butter or margarine
2 tablespoons HERSHEY'S Cocoa
2 tablespoons water
1 cup powdered sugar
½ teaspoon vanilla extract

1. For Chocolate Sponge Roll, heat oven to 375°F. Line 15½×10½×1-inch jelly-roll pan with foil; generously grease foil.

2. Beat egg whites in large bowl with electric mixer on high speed until soft peaks form; gradually add ½ cup granulated sugar, beating until stiff peaks form. Set aside.

3. Beat egg yolks and vanilla in medium bowl with electric mixer on medium speed 3 minutes. Gradually add remaining ⅓ cup granulated sugar; continue beating 2 minutes. Stir together flour, cocoa, baking powder, baking soda and salt. With mixer on low speed, add flour mixture to egg yolk mixture alternately with water, beating just until batter is smooth. Using rubber spatula, gradually fold beaten egg whites into chocolate mixture until well blended. Spread batter evenly in prepared pan.

4. Bake 12 to 15 minutes or until top springs back when touched lightly. Immediately loosen cake from edges of pan; invert onto clean towel sprinkled with powdered sugar. Carefully peel off foil. Immediately roll cake in towel, starting from narrow end; place on wire rack to cool completely.

5. For Peppermint Filling, beat whipping cream in medium bowl with electric mixer on medium speed until slightly thickened. Add ¼ cup powdered sugar, peppermint candy and food coloring, if desired; beat until stiff peaks form.

6. For Chocolate Glaze, melt butter in small saucepan over very low heat; add cocoa and water, stirring until smooth and slightly thickened. Remove from heat and cool slightly. (Cool completely for thicker glaze.) Gradually beat in 1 cup powdered sugar and vanilla extract.

7. Carefully unroll cake; remove towel. Spread cake with Peppermint Filling; reroll cake. Glaze with Chocolate Glaze. Refrigerate until just before serving. Cover and refrigerate leftover cake roll.

Makes 10 to 12 servings

Variation: Substitute Coffee Filling for Peppermint Filling. Combine 1½ cups cold milk and 2 teaspoons instant coffee granules in medium bowl; let stand 5 minutes. Add 1 package (4-serving size) instant vanilla pudding. Beat with electric mixer on lowest speed about 2 minutes or until well blended. Use as directed above to fill Chocolate Sponge Roll.

Buche De Noel Cookies

⅔ cup butter or margarine, softened
1 cup granulated sugar
2 eggs
2 teaspoons vanilla extract
2½ cups all-purpose flour
½ cup HERSHEY₅S Cocoa
½ teaspoon baking soda
¼ teaspoon salt
    Mocha Frosting (recipe follows)
    Powdered sugar (optional)

1. Beat butter and sugar in large bowl with electric mixer on medium speed until well blended. Add eggs and vanilla; beat until fluffy. Stir together flour, cocoa, baking soda and salt; gradually add to butter mixture, beating until well blended. Cover and refrigerate dough 1 to 2 hours.

2. Heat oven to 350°F. Shape heaping teaspoons of dough into logs about 2½ inches long and ¾ inches in diameter; place on ungreased cookie sheet. Bake 7 to 9 minutes or until set. Cool slightly. Remove to wire rack and cool completely.

3. Frost cookies with Mocha Frosting. Using tines of fork, draw lines through frosting to imitate tree bark. Lightly dust with powdered sugar, if desired.   *Makes about 2½ dozen cookies*

Mocha Frosting

6 tablespoons butter or margarine, softened

2⅔ cups powdered sugar

⅓ cup HERSHEY'S Cocoa

3 to 4 tablespoons milk

2 teaspoons powdered instant espresso dissolved in
1 teaspoon hot water

1 teaspoon vanilla extract

HELPFUL HINT

Instant espresso powder is a great thing to keep on hand. It really helps to bring out the rich flavor of the cocoa.

Beat butter in medium bowl with electric mixer on medium speed until creamy. Add powdered sugar and cocoa alternately with milk, dissolved espresso and vanilla, beating to spreadable consistency.

Makes about 1⅔ cups frosting

Peanut Butter and Milk Chocolate Chip Mud Balls

1 cup HERSHEY'S Milk Chocolate Chips, divided
1 cup REESE'S® Peanut Butter Chips, divided
½ teaspoon shortening (do not use butter, margarine, spread or oil)

1. Stir together milk chocolate chips and peanut butter chips. Coarsely chop 1⅓ cups chip mixture in food processor or by hand; place in medium bowl.

2. Place remaining ⅔ cup chip mixture and shortening in small microwave-safe bowl. Microwave at HIGH (100%) 45 seconds; stir. If necessary, microwave at HIGH an additional 15 seconds at a time, stirring after each heating, until chips are melted and mixture is smooth.

3. Pour melted chocolate mixture over chopped chips; stir to coat evenly. With hands, form mixture into 1-inch balls. Place in small candy cups, if desired. Store in cool, dry place. **Makes about 20 candies**

Cranberry Orange Ricotta Cheese Brownies

½ cup (1 stick) butter or margarine, melted
¾ cup sugar
1 teaspoon vanilla extract
2 eggs
¾ cup all-purpose flour
½ cup HERSHEY'S Cocoa
½ teaspoon *each* baking powder and salt
Cheese Filling (recipe follows)

1. Heat oven to 350°F. Grease 9-inch square baking pan. Prepare cheese filling.

2. Stir together butter, sugar and vanilla in medium bowl; add eggs, beating well. Stir together flour, cocoa, baking powder and salt; add to butter mixture, mixing thoroughly. Spread half of chocolate batter in prepared pan. Spread Cheese Filling over top. Drop remaining chocolate batter by teaspoons onto cheese filling.

3. Bake 40 to 45 minutes or until wooden pick inserted into center comes out clean. Cool completely in pan on wire rack. Cut into squares. Refrigerate leftover brownies.   ***Makes about 16 brownies***

Cheese Filling

1 cup ricotta cheese
¼ cup sugar
3 tablespoons whole-berry cranberry sauce
2 tablespoons cornstarch
1 egg
¼ to ½ teaspoon freshly grated orange peel

Beat ricotta cheese, sugar, cranberry sauce, cornstarch and egg in small bowl until smooth. Stir in orange peel.

Peanut Butter and Milk Chocolate Chip Mud Balls

Viennese Chocolate Torte

¼ cup HERSHEY'S Cocoa
¼ cup boiling water
¾ cup sugar
⅓ cup shortening
½ teaspoon vanilla extract
 1 egg
 1 cup all-purpose flour
¾ teaspoon baking soda
¼ teaspoon salt
⅔ cup buttermilk or sour milk*
¼ cup seedless black raspberry preserves
 Cream Filling (recipe follows)
 Cocoa Glaze (recipe follows)
 MOUNDS® Coconut Flakes, toasted

To sour milk: Use 2 teaspoons white vinegar plus milk to equal ⅔ cup.

1. Heat oven to 350°F. Lightly grease 15½×10½×1-inch jelly-roll pan; line pan with wax paper and lightly grease paper.

2. Stir together cocoa and boiling water in small bowl until smooth; set aside. Beat sugar, shortening and vanilla in medium bowl until creamy; beat in egg. Stir together flour, baking soda and salt; add alternately with buttermilk to shortening mixture. Add reserved cocoa mixture, beating just until blended. Spread batter in pan.

3. Bake 16 to 18 minutes or until wooden pick inserted into center comes out clean. Cool 10 minutes; remove from pan. Remove wax paper; cool completely. Cut cake crosswise into three equal pieces. Place one piece on serving plate; spread 2 tablespoons preserves evenly over cake layer. Spread half of Cream Filling over preserves. Repeat layering. Glaze top of torte with Cocoa Glaze, allowing some to drizzle down sides. Garnish with coconut. Refrigerate several hours. Cover and refrigerate leftover torte. *Makes 10 to 12 servings*

Cream Filling: Beat 1 cup whipping cream, 2 tablespoons powdered sugar and 1 teaspoon vanilla in small bowl until stiff. Makes about 2 cups filling.

Cocoa Glaze

2 tablespoons butter or margarine
2 tablespoons HERSHEY'S Cocoa
2 tablespoons water
1 cup powdered sugar
½ teaspoon vanilla extract

Melt butter in saucepan. Stir in cocoa and water. Cook, stirring constantly, until mixture thickens. (Do not boil.) Remove from heat. Gradually whisk in powdered sugar. Add vanilla and beat with whisk until smooth. Add additional water, ½ teaspoon at a time, until desired consistency.

Truffles make wonderful holiday gifts. Arrange truffles in small paper cups in pretty paper boxes for a beautiful presentation.

Special Dark™ Fudge Truffles

2 cups (12-ounce package) HERSHEY'S SPECIAL DARK™ Chocolate Chips
¾ cup whipping cream
    Various coatings such as toasted chopped pecans, coconut, powdered sugar, cocoa or small candy pieces

1. Combine chocolate chips and whipping cream in medium microwave-safe bowl. Microwave at HIGH (100%) 1 minute; stir. If necessary, microwave an additional 15 seconds at a time, stirring after each heating, until chips are melted and mixture is smooth when stirred.

2. Refrigerate 3 hours or until firm. Shape mixture into 1-inch balls. Roll each ball in coating. Cover and refrigerate leftover candies.

Makes about 3 dozen truffles

Cheery Cheesecake Cookie Bars

1 package (4 ounces) HERSHEY'S Unsweetened Chocolate Premium Baking Bar, broken into pieces
1 cup (2 sticks) butter
2½ cups sugar, divided
4 eggs, divided
1 teaspoon vanilla extract
2 cups all-purpose flour
1 package (8 ounces) cream cheese, softened
1¾ cups (10-ounce package) HERSHEY'S MINI KISSES® BRAND Milk Chocolates, divided
½ cup chopped red or green maraschino cherries
½ teaspoon almond extract
    Few drops red food coloring (optional)

1. Heat oven to 350°F. Grease 13×9×2-inch baking pan.

Cheery Cheesecake Cookie Bar

2. Place unsweetened chocolate and butter in large microwave-safe bowl. Microwave at HIGH (100%) 2 minutes, stirring after each minute, until chocolate is melted and mixture is smooth. Beat in 2 cups sugar, 3 eggs and vanilla until blended. Stir in flour; spread batter in prepared pan.

3. Beat cream cheese, remaining ½ cup sugar and remaining 1 egg; stir in 1¼ cups chocolates, cherries, almond extract and food coloring, if desired. Drop by spoonfuls over top of chocolate mixture in pan.

4. Bake 35 to 40 minutes or just until set. Remove from oven; immediately sprinkle remaining ½ cup chocolates over top. Cool completely in pan on wire rack; cut into bars. Cover and refrigerate leftover bars. *Makes 3 dozen bars*

Holiday Coconut Cake

COCONUT CAKE

½ cup (1 stick) butter or margarine, softened

2 cups sugar

½ cup shortening

5 eggs, separated

1 teaspoon vanilla extract

2 cups all-purpose flour

1 teaspoon baking soda

¼ teaspoon salt

1 cup buttermilk or sour milk*

2 cups MOUNDS® Sweetened Coconut Flakes

½ cup chopped pecans

TOFFEE CREAM

2 cups cold whipping cream

¼ cup powdered sugar

1 teaspoon vanilla extract

½ cup HEATH® BITS 'O BRICKLE® Toffee Bits

Additional HEATH® BITS 'O BRICKLE® Toffee Bits (optional)

To sour milk: Use 2 teaspoons white vinegar plus milk to equal ⅔ cup.

1. Heat oven to 350°F. Grease and flour 12-cup fluted tube pan.

2. Beat butter, sugar, shortening, egg yolks and vanilla in large bowl with electric mixer on medium speed until creamy. Stir together flour, baking soda and salt; add alternately with buttermilk, beating until well blended. Stir in coconut and pecans.

3. Beat egg whites in separate large bowl with electric mixer on high speed until stiff peaks form; fold into batter. Pour batter into prepared pan.

4. Bake 45 to 55 minutes or until wooden pick inserted near center comes out clean. Cool 10 minutes; remove from pan to wire rack. Cool completely.

Holiday Coconut Cake

5. For Toffee Cream, beat whipping cream, powdered sugar and vanilla in large bowl with electric mixer on medium speed until stiff peaks form. Fold in toffee bits. Frost cake with Toffee Cream. Garnish with additional toffee bits, if desired. Cover and refrigerate leftover cake.   *Makes 10 to 12 servings*

BREADS
& MUFFINS

Peanut Butter and Milk Chocolate Chip Crescents

¼ cup HERSHEY'S Milk Chocolate Chips
¼ cup REESE'S® Peanut Butter Chips
2 tablespoons finely chopped nuts
1 can (8 ounces) refrigerated quick crescent dinner rolls
Powdered sugar

1. Heat oven to 375°F.

2. Stir together milk chocolate chips, peanut butter chips and nuts in small bowl. Unroll dough to form 8 triangles. Sprinkle 1 heaping tablespoon chip mixture on top of each triangle; gently press into dough. Starting at shortest side of triangle, roll dough to opposite point. Place rolls, point side down, on ungreased cookie sheet; curve into crescent shape.

3. Bake 10 to 12 minutes or until golden brown. Sprinkle with powdered sugar. Serve warm. *Makes 8 crescents*

These crescents make a terrific sweet breakfast treat and an even better simple dessert.

Peanut Butter and Milk Chocolate Chip Crescents

Cinnamon Chip Applesauce Coffeecake

1 cup (2 sticks) butter or margarine, softened
1 cup granulated sugar
2 eggs
½ teaspoon vanilla extract
¾ cup applesauce
2½ cups all-purpose flour
1 teaspoon baking soda
½ teaspoon salt
1⅔ cups (10-ounce package) HERSHEY'S Cinnamon Chips
1 cup chopped pecans (optional)
¾ cup powdered sugar
1 to 2 tablespoons warm water

1. Heat oven to 350°F. Lightly grease 13×9×2-inch baking pan.

2. Beat butter and sugar in large bowl with electric mixer on medium speed until well blended. Beat in eggs and vanilla. Stir in applesauce. Stir together flour, baking soda and salt; gradually add to butter mixture, beating until well blended. Stir in cinnamon chips and pecans, if desired. Spread evenly in prepared pan.

3. Bake 30 to 35 minutes or until wooden pick inserted into center comes out clean. Cool in pan on wire rack. Stir together powdered sugar and warm water to make smooth glaze; drizzle over cake. Serve warm or at room temperature. *Makes 12 to 15 servings*

Fluted Cake: Grease and flour 12-cup fluted tube pan. Prepare batter as directed; pour into prepared pan. Bake 45 to 50 minutes or until wooden pick inserted near center comes out clean. Cool 15 minutes; invert onto wire rack. Cool completely.

Cinnamon Chip Applesauce Coffeecake

Cupcakes: Line 24 standard (2½-inch) baking cups with paper liners. Prepare batter as directed; divide evenly into prepared cups. Bake 15 to 18 minutes or until wooden pick inserted into centers comes out clean. Cool completely.

Star-of-the-East Fruit Bread

½ cup (1 stick) butter or margarine, softened
1 cup sugar
2 eggs
1 teaspoon vanilla extract
2 cups all-purpose flour
1 teaspoon baking soda
¼ teaspoon salt
1 cup mashed ripe bananas (about 3 medium)
1 can (11 ounces) mandarin orange segments, well-drained
1 cup HERSHEY'S Semi-Sweet Chocolate Chips
½ cup chopped dates or Calimyrna figs
½ cup chopped maraschino cherries, well-drained
  Chocolate Drizzle (recipe follows)

1. Heat oven to 350°F. Grease two 8½×4½×2⅝-inch loaf pans.

2. Beat butter and sugar in large bowl until fluffy. Add eggs and vanilla; beat well. Stir together flour, baking soda and salt; add alternately with mashed bananas to butter mixture, blending well. Stir in orange segments, chocolate chips, dates and cherries. Divide batter evenly between prepared pans.

3. Bake 40 to 50 minutes or until golden brown. Cool; remove from pans. Drizzle tops of loaves with Chocolate Drizzle. Store tightly wrapped at room temperature. *Makes 2 loaves*

Chocolate Drizzle: Combine ½ cup HERSHEY'S Semi-Sweet Chocolate Chips and 2 tablespoons whipping cream in small microwave-safe bowl. Microwave at HIGH (100%) 30 seconds; stir. If necessary, microwave at HIGH an additional 15 seconds; stir until chips are melted and mixture is smooth when stirred. Makes about ½ cup.

Don't stir muffin batter too much—overmixing will make muffins tough. There should still be lumps in the batter; these will disappear during baking.

Peanut Butter Chip & Banana Mini Muffins

2 cups all-purpose biscuit baking mix
¼ cup sugar
2 tablespoons butter or margarine, softened
1 egg
1 cup mashed ripe bananas (2 to 3 medium)
1 cup REESE'S® Peanut Butter Chips
Quick Glaze (recipe follows, optional)

1. Heat oven to 400°F. Grease mini (1¾ inch) muffin cups.

2. Stir together baking mix, sugar, butter and egg in medium bowl; with fork, beat vigorously for 30 seconds. Stir in bananas and peanut butter chips. Fill muffin cups two-thirds full with batter.

3. Bake 12 to 15 minutes or until golden brown. Meanwhile, prepare Quick Glaze, if desired. Immediately remove muffins from pan; dip tops of warm muffins into glaze. Serve warm.

Makes about 4 dozen small muffins

Quick Glaze

1½ cups powdered sugar
2 tablespoons water

Stir together powdered sugar and water in small bowl until smooth and of desired consistency. Add additional water, ½ teaspoon at a time, if needed.

Orange Chocolate Chip Bread

Orange Chocolate Chip Bread

½ cup nonfat milk

½ cup plain nonfat yogurt

⅓ cup sugar

¼ cup orange juice

1 egg, slightly beaten

1 tablespoon freshly grated orange peel

3 cups all-purpose biscuit baking mix

½ cup HERSHEY₅'S MINI CHIPS™ Semi-Sweet Chocolate Chips

1. Heat oven to 350°F. Grease 9×5×3-inch loaf pan or spray with vegetable cooking spray.

2. Stir together milk, yogurt, sugar, orange juice, egg and orange peel in large bowl; add baking mix. Beat until well combined. Stir in chocolate chips. Pour into prepared pan.

3. Bake 45 to 50 minutes or until wooden pick inserted into center comes out clean. Cool 10 minutes; remove from pan to wire rack. Cool completely before slicing. Garnish as desired. Wrap leftover bread in foil or plastic wrap. Store tightly wrapped at room temperature or freeze for longer storage.   ***Makes 1 loaf (16 slices)***

Cocoa Cherry-Nut Snacking Bread

½ cup (1 stick) butter or margarine, softened

1 cup sugar

2 eggs

1 cup buttermilk or sour milk*

1¾ cups all-purpose flour

½ cup HERSHEY₀S Cocoa

½ teaspoon baking powder

½ teaspoon baking soda

¼ teaspoon salt

½ cup finely chopped walnuts

½ cup finely chopped maraschino cherries, drained

    Easy Vanilla Glaze (recipe follows, optional)

    Maraschino cherries, halved (optional)

    Walnut halves (optional)

To sour milk: Use 1 tablespoon white vinegar plus milk to equal 1 cup.

1. Heat oven to 350°F. Grease bottom only of 9×5×3-inch loaf pan.

2. Beat butter, sugar and eggs in large bowl until well blended. Stir in buttermilk. Stir together flour, cocoa, baking powder, baking soda and salt; gradually add to butter mixture, beating well. Stir in chopped walnuts and chopped cherries. Pour batter into prepared pan.

3. Bake 55 to 60 minutes or until wooden pick inserted into center comes out clean. (Bread will crack slightly in center.) Cool 15 minutes. Remove from pan to wire rack. Cool completely.

4. Prepare Easy Vanilla Glaze, if desired; drizzle over bread. Garnish with cherry halves and walnut halves, if desired.

Makes about 12 servings

Easy Vanilla Glaze

1 tablespoon butter or margarine
½ cup powdered sugar
2 teaspoons hot water

Place butter in small microwave-safe bowl. Microwave at HIGH (100%) 30 seconds or until melted. Add powdered sugar. Gradually add water; stir until smooth and of desired consistency. Add additional water, ½ teaspoon at a time, if needed.

Chocolate Quicky Sticky Bread

2 loaves (16 ounces each) frozen bread dough
¾ cup granulated sugar
1 tablespoon HERSHEY'S Cocoa
1 teaspoon ground cinnamon
½ cup (1 stick) butter or margarine, melted and divided
½ cup packed light brown sugar
¼ cup water
    HERSHEY'S MINI KISSES® BRAND Milk Chocolates

1. Thaw loaves as directed on package; let rise until doubled.

2. Stir together granulated sugar, cocoa and cinnamon. Stir together ¼ cup butter, brown sugar and water in small microwave-safe bowl. Microwave at HIGH (100%) 30 to 60 seconds or until smooth when stirred. Pour mixture into 12-cup fluted tube pan.

3. Heat oven to 350°F. Pinch off pieces of bread dough; form into balls 1½ inches in diameter, placing 3 chocolates inside each ball. Dip each ball in remaining ¼ cup butter; roll in cocoa-sugar mixture. Place balls in prepared pan.

4. Bake 45 to 50 minutes or until golden brown. Cool 20 minutes in pan; invert onto serving plate. Cool until lukewarm.

Makes 12 servings

To reheat leftover scones, place on a microwave-safe plate. Microwave on HIGH (100%) 15 to 20 seconds or until warm.

Tropical Paradise Scones

3 1/4 cups all-purpose flour

1/2 cup sugar

1 tablespoon plus 1 teaspoon baking powder

1/4 teaspoon salt

1 1/3 cups (8-ounce package) HERSHEY'S White Chips and Macadamia Nuts

1 cup MOUNDS® Sweetened Coconut Flakes

2 cups cold whipping cream

2 tablespoons fresh lime juice

2 to 3 teaspoons freshly grated lime peel

2 tablespoons butter, melted

Additional sugar

1. Heat oven to 375°F. Lightly grease 2 baking sheets.

2. Stir together flour, 1/2 cup sugar, baking powder and salt in large bowl. Stir in chips, nuts and coconut. Stir whipping cream, lime juice and lime peel into flour mixture, stirring just until ingredients are moistened.

3. Turn mixture out onto lightly floured surface. Knead gently until soft dough forms (about 2 minutes). Divide dough into three equal balls. One ball at a time, flatten into 7-inch circle; cut into 8 triangles. Transfer triangles to prepared baking sheets, spacing 2 inches apart. Brush with melted butter and sprinkle with additional sugar.

4. Bake 15 to 20 minutes or until lightly browned. Serve warm or at room temperature. ***Makes 24 scones***

Quick Cinnamon Sticky Buns

1 cup packed light brown sugar, divided
10 tablespoons butter, softened and divided
1 package (16-ounce) hot roll mix
2 tablespoons granulated sugar
1 cup hot water (120° to 130°F)
1 egg
1⅔ cups (10-ounce package) HERSHEY'S Cinnamon Chips

1. Lightly grease two 9-inch round baking pans. Combine ½ cup brown sugar and 4 tablespoons softened butter in small bowl with pastry blender; sprinkle mixture evenly on bottom of prepared pans. Set aside.

2. Combine contents of hot roll mix package including yeast packet and granulated sugar in large bowl. Stir in water, 2 tablespoons butter and egg until dough pulls away from sides of bowl. Turn dough onto lightly floured surface. With lightly floured hands, shape into ball. Knead 5 minutes or until smooth, using additional flour if necessary.

3. Using lightly floured rolling pin, roll into 15×12-inch rectangle. Spread with remaining 4 tablespoons butter. Sprinkle with remaining ½ cup brown sugar and cinnamon chips, pressing lightly into dough. Starting with 12-inch side, roll tightly as for jelly roll; seal edges.

4. Cut into 1-inch-wide slices with floured knife. Arrange 6 slices, cut sides down, in each prepared pan. Cover with towel; let rise in warm place until doubled, about 30 minutes.

5. Heat oven to 350°F. Uncover rolls. Bake 25 to 30 minutes or until golden brown. Cool 2 minutes in pan; with knife, loosen around edge of pan. Invert onto serving plates. Serve warm or at room temperature.

Makes 12 cinnamon buns

If fresh cranberries are unavailable, frozen will work just fine. During cranberry season, throw a few bags in your freezer to use all year long.

Berry Loaf

2 cups all-purpose flour
1 cup sugar
1½ teaspoons baking powder
1 teaspoon salt
½ teaspoon baking soda
¾ cup orange juice
1 teaspoon freshly grated orange peel
2 tablespoons shortening
1 egg, slightly beaten
1 cup chopped fresh cranberries
1 cup HERSHEY'S MINI CHIPS™ Semi-Sweet Chocolate Chips
¾ cup chopped nuts
Powdered Sugar Glaze (recipe follows, optional)

1. Heat oven to 350°F. Grease 9×5×3-inch loaf pan.

2. Stir together flour, sugar, baking powder, salt and baking soda in large bowl. Add orange juice, orange peel, shortening and egg; stir until well blended. Stir in cranberries, chocolate chips and nuts. Pour batter into prepared pan.

3. Bake 1 hour 5 minutes to 1 hour 10 minutes or until wooden pick inserted into center comes out clean. Cool 10 minutes; remove from pan to wire rack. Prepare Powdered Sugar Glaze, if desired; spread over top of loaf. Cool completely. Garnish as desired.

Makes 1 loaf (14 servings)

Powdered Sugar Glaze

1 cup powdered sugar
1 tablespoon milk
1 teaspoon butter or margarine, softened
½ teaspoon vanilla extract

(left to right): Cocoa Cherry-Nut Snacking Bread (page 112) and Berry Loaf

Stir together powdered sugar, milk, butter and vanilla in small bowl; beat until smooth and of desired consistency. Add additional milk, 1 teaspoon at a time, if needed.   *Makes about ½ cup glaze*

White Chip and Macadamia Nut Coffeecake

Crumb Topping (recipe follows)
6 tablespoons butter or margarine, softened
¾ cup granulated sugar
¾ cup packed light brown sugar
2 cups all-purpose flour
2 teaspoons baking powder
½ teaspoon ground cinnamon
1¼ cups milk
1 egg
1 teaspoon vanilla extract
White Drizzle (recipe follows)

1. Heat oven to 350°F. Grease and flour 13×9×2-inch baking pan. Prepare Crumb Topping; set aside.

2. Beat butter, granulated sugar and brown sugar until well blended. Stir together flour, baking powder and cinnamon; beat into butter mixture. Gradually add milk, egg and vanilla, beating until thoroughly blended. Pour ½ batter into prepared pan; top with ½ Crumb Topping. Gently spread remaining batter over topping. Sprinkle remaining topping over batter.

3. Bake 30 to 35 minutes or until wooden pick inserted into center comes out clean. Cool completely.

4. Prepare White Drizzle; drizzle over cake.   *Makes 12 to 16 servings*

Crumb Topping: Combine 1⅓ cups (8-ounce package) HERSHEY'S Premier White Chips and Macadamia Nuts, ⅔ cup packed light brown sugar, ½ cup all-purpose flour and 6 tablespoons cold butter or margarine in medium bowl. Mix until crumbly.

White Chip and Macadamia Nut Coffeecake

White Drizzle: Beat together ¾ cup powdered sugar, 2 teaspoons milk, 1 teaspoon softened butter and ¼ teaspoon vanilla extract. If necessary, stir in additional milk ½ teaspoon at a time until desired consistency.

Index

Metric Conversion Chart

VOLUME MEASUREMENTS (dry)

¹/₈ teaspoon = 0.5 mL
¹/₄ teaspoon = 1 mL
¹/₂ teaspoon = 2 mL
³/₄ teaspoon = 4 mL
1 teaspoon = 5 mL
1 tablespoon = 15 mL
2 tablespoons = 30 mL
¹/₄ cup = 60 mL
¹/₃ cup = 75 mL
¹/₂ cup = 125 mL
²/₃ cup = 150 mL
³/₄ cup = 175 mL
1 cup = 250 mL
2 cups = 1 pint = 500 mL
3 cups = 750 mL
4 cups = 1 quart = 1 L

VOLUME MEASUREMENTS (fluid)

1 fluid ounce (2 tablespoons) = 30 mL
4 fluid ounces (¹/₂ cup) = 125 mL
8 fluid ounces (1 cup) = 250 mL
12 fluid ounces (1¹/₂ cups) = 375 mL
16 fluid ounces (2 cups) = 500 mL

WEIGHTS (mass)

¹/₂ ounce = 15 g
1 ounce = 30 g
3 ounces = 90 g
4 ounces = 120 g
8 ounces = 225 g
10 ounces = 285 g
12 ounces = 360 g
16 ounces = 1 pound = 450 g

DIMENSIONS

¹/₁₆ inch = 2 mm
¹/₈ inch = 3 mm
¹/₄ inch = 6 mm
¹/₂ inch = 1.5 cm
³/₄ inch = 2 cm
1 inch = 2.5 cm

OVEN TEMPERATURES

250°F = 120°C
275°F = 140°C
300°F = 150°C
325°F = 160°C
350°F = 180°C
375°F = 190°C
400°F = 200°C
425°F = 220°C
450°F = 230°C

BAKING PAN SIZES

Utensil	Size in Inches/Quarts	Metric Volume	Size in Centimeters
Baking or Cake Pan (square or rectangular)	8×8×2	2 L	20×20×5
	9×9×2	2.5 L	23×23×5
	12×8×2	3 L	30×20×5
	13×9×2	3.5 L	33×23×5
Loaf Pan	8×4×3	1.5 L	20×10×7
	9×5×3	2 L	23×13×7
Round Layer Cake Pan	8×1½	1.2 L	20×4
	9×1½	1.5 L	23×4
Pie Plate	8×1¼	750 mL	20×3
	9×1¼	1 L	23×3
Baking Dish or Casserole	1 quart	1 L	—
	1½ quart	1.5 L	—
	2 quart	2 L	—